Strategic Intelligence for Law Firms

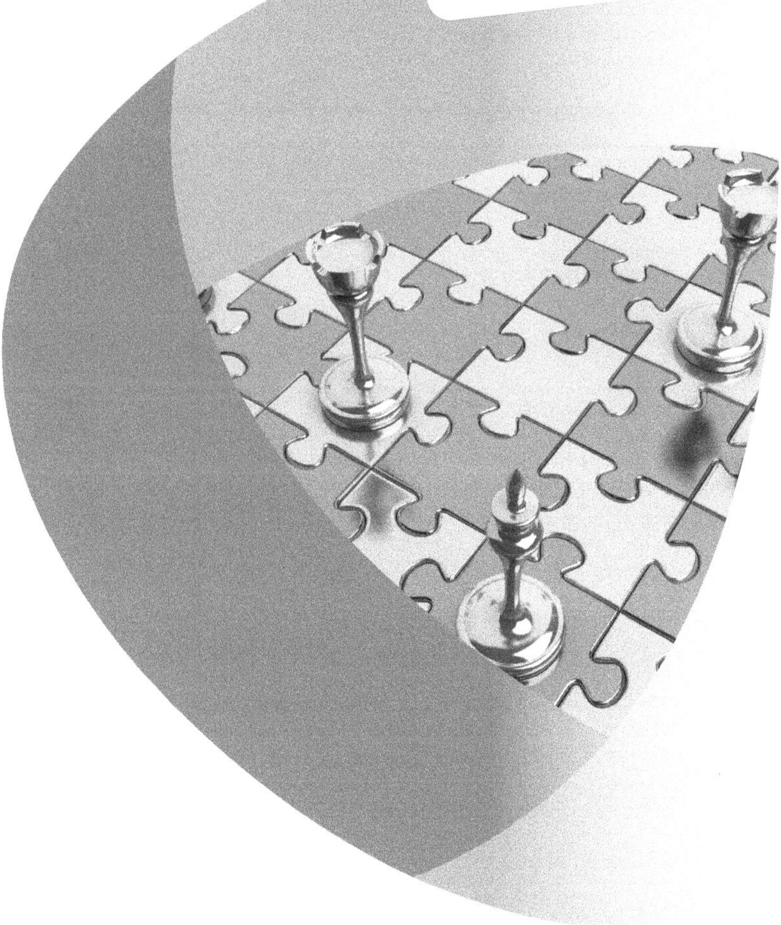

EDITED BY LAURA SLATER

Head of events and books
Leah Darbyshire

Commissioning editor
Laura Slater

Editorial assistant
Edward Bowes

Published by
Globe Law and Business Ltd
3 Mylor Close
Horsell
Woking
Surrey GU21 4DD
United Kingdom
Tel: +44 20 3745 4770
www.globelawandbusiness.com

ISBN: 978-1-78358-240-2
A catalogue record for this book is available from the British Library

Contents

Executive summary vii

About the authors ix

Chapter 1: Client success through better intelligence 1
By Mark Medice, senior director, and Jennifer Roberts, senior analyst at Intapp Client Success
State of the industry 2
Client intelligence opportunity 3
Data-driven and systematic approaches 3
Measurement, insights, and action 6
Cultural considerations 9
Managing progress in light of the larger vision 9
Summary 10

Chapter 2: Why client intelligence is (or should be) the new CI for law firms 13
By Zena Applebaum, director of competitive intelligence at Bennett Jones LLP
The CI cycle 13
And then it was 2008 – An industry in flux 14
Technology makes it easy 16
Understand my business 17
Collaboration is the key to client intelligence 21

Chapter 3: Balancing pricing and client perceptions of value 23
By Peter Lane-Secor, director of strategic pricing and project management at Pepper Hamilton LLP
Defining value 23
Using communications to demonstrate value 25
Estimates and fee structures 27

Chapter 4: Utilizing multiple intelligence sources to create an opportunity scoring assessment 33
By Patrick Fuller, vice president of business development for Neota Logic, Inc.
Setting the foundations – Metrics and scope 33
Legal intelligence platforms 34
Relationships and connections 36
Experience 37
Finance, pricing, and profitability 38

Chapter 5: Developing a CI function in a resource-constrained environment 41
By Annie Johnson, manager of business intelligence at Pillsbury Winthrop Shaw Pittman
Gaining buy-in 41
Process, process, process 42
People 43
Take initiative 44
Solicit and implement feedback 44
Track outcomes 45
Ready to launch 46

Chapter 6: Compiling a useful and user-friendly competitive intelligence report 49
By Mark A. Gediman, director of information services at Best Best & Krieger LLP
Step 1 – Choice of format 49
Step 2 – The executive summary 50
Step 3 – Establish the purpose of the report 51
Step 4 – Tools 53
Conclusion 55

Chapter 7: Design Thinking and the ***why*** of BI 57
By John Alber, futurist at the International Legal Technology Association
Change or die 57
But change how? 59
Design thinking discipline 59
Empathy? 60
Bringing empathy to BI 61
OMG 63
Beginning with the prosaic 64
Back to the why of BI 66

Chapter 8: From BI to AI 69
By Joanna Goodman, freelance journalist and IT columnist; author of Robots in Law *(ARK Group, 2016)*
BI and big data 70
AI's two-factor authentication 72
The AI of BI – and the BI of AI! 74
Get the BI right first 75
From dashboard to conversation 76

Chapter 9: URLs or UPL? Using software to close the access to justice gap 77
By Ed Walters, CEO of Fastcase, and Jeffrey Asjes, research and reference attorney at Fastcase
Mind the gap 78
A history of software turbulence 78
Legal software is already here 79
Industry concerns 80
What's next 81
Unauthorized practice of law 81
Unclear boundaries 81
Inputs vs outputs 83
A future of robots in the law 84
Lawyers in the loop 85
Quality service at scale 86
Colophon 86

Executive summary

Research and data are now a firm's best tools in garnering and retaining business. Having a comprehensive knowledge of not only your client's needs in terms of your business, but also of the greater workings outside your terms of engagement is the best route to offering quality and value-oriented services. But with the modern, techno-centric world offering up an endless supply of data, and a multitude of ways to collect it, what is the best method of implementing this shift in focus?

Strategic Intelligence for Law Firms offers a robust overview of how, and *why*, strategic use of intelligence can foster real results in your firm. Featuring advice and case studies from experts in business development; analytics; and the ABC of artificial, business, and competitive intelligence, the book leads with defining the true nature and worth of competitive intelligence, and develops into discussing methods of deploying, demonstrating, and utilizing intelligence to its full potential.

The book opens with a chapter from Mark Medice and Jennifer Roberts of Intapp, who summarize how firms can use client intelligence to create and maintain advantage, the profits and savings that can be accomplished, and how the cultural shift to a client-focused environment can be implemented in a sector that is notoriously adverse to change. In Chapter 2 Zena Applebaum, director of competitive intelligence at Bennett Jones LLP, explains how client-focused intelligence is now the standard for all competitive intelligence – and what is fundamentally different in this shift. Details are given on how research on clients can progress into client retention, especially as clients now have an increasing number of options to choose from, and are looking for greater value for money. Keeping on the topic of value, Chapter 3 features Pepper Hamilton LLP's director of strategic pricing and project management, Peter Lane Secor, discussing how differing definitions of "value" can create dissatisfaction within the client. Advice is given on how to structure fees and estimates to promote value, and when "going the extra mile" may be disproportionate and inappropriate in the context.

With all the effort required to collect and collate data, firms want to ensure that the intelligence is applied correctly for real results. In Chapter 4 the vice president of business development at Neota Logic Inc., Patrick Fuller, discusses the best ways to fully utilize intelligence gathered from a number of sources. The core principles of developing an opportunity scoring assessment are outlined – a system of quantifying all internal resources to ensure that they are applied correctly and efficiently. Chapter 5 sees Annie Johnson, manager of business intelligence for Pillsbury Winthrop Shaw Pittman, tackling an issue which is now critical for many law firms: how to capitalize on the shift towards CI with a limited set of resources. The chapter outlines all the steps needed to launch an effective CI department: calculating the demand; creating the processes; finding appropriate staff; and pitching it to the workforce.

Any collected data is, however, only as effective as the method chosen to present it. In Chapter 6 Mark A. Gediman, director of information services at Best Best & Krieger LLP, offers a detailed lesson in building the perfect report to deliver crucial data – while keeping it engaging and user-friendly. Effective methods of presenting data are discussed, and advice is given on which style of report would best represent the kind of data at hand – along with standard steps to ensure that your reports stand out.

In Chapter 7 John Alber discusses the fundamentals of business intelligence in order to highlight the reason of *why* BI is undertaken and, more importantly, why it is a key to success. He then outlines the process of "Design Thinking", and how it can be used to help firms evolve their business in the right direction – by questioning and defining the most basic operations of a firm. As developments in technology steadily progress, the question of how firms will interact with and utilize high-end technology to augment their intelligence functions is becoming a key subject for debate. Chapter 8 features Joanna Goodman discussing the potential of BI to create value via data capture and analysis, leading into how future developments can lead to "legal AI", what its core functions will be, and how it can work in tandem with BI functions. Chapter 9 begins with Ed Walters and Jeff Asjes of Fastcase outlining how software can be implemented to increase access to legal services, and discusses the legal implications of such software in regard to unauthorised practice of law statutes.

About the authors

John Alber serves as futurist for the International Legal Technology Association. He also writes, speaks, and consults, focusing on finding practical ways to reshape the delivery of legal services to suit a future demanding excellence far beyond substantive legal skills.

Prior to his current role, John led Bryan Cave LLP to become one of the most innovative firms in the world, serving as its Strategic Innovation Partner for more than 16 years. While at Bryan Cave, he also served for seven years on the firm's Operating Group (its management committee).

At Bryan Cave, John created one of the first Practice Economics consulting groups, one of the first client facing technology groups and one of the first in-firm legal process outsourcing (LPO) organizations. The groups he created developed innovative web-based, client-centric applications that delivered legal advice to clients, managed complex workflows and even created pleadings automatically. They also developed client-facing knowledge management, project management, project estimation, and business intelligence systems and highly technology-leveraged alternative staffing solutions for engagements of all types.

John has written and spoken widely on legal innovation subjects and received a number of awards, both in the legal field and in information technology generally. Among other awards, he received ILTA's first ever Premiership Award, was named American Lawyer Media's first ever 'Champion of Technology', was given a Lifetime Achievement Award by Law Technology News, and was recognized as one of the 'Top 25 CTOs' in the world by Infoworld. In addition, while under his leadership, Bryan Cave received recognition as a CIO Magazine 'Top 100 Company' and was twice recognized as ILTA's Most Innovative Firm.

Zena Applebaum is the director of competitive intelligence at Bennett Jones LLP, an international law firm based in Canada. Zena's primary responsibilities include business and practice development, market and competitor performance analysis, client relationship management, counter-intelligence and marketing. Zena brings a unique perspective to intelligence as a result of broad business development, data management, marketing, and corporate research experience in a variety of sectors. Zena has a joint academic and applied Master of Arts degree in Communication and Culture from York and Ryerson Universities. A regular speaker, writer and blogger on competitive intelligence topics in Canada and abroad, Zena authored *Business Intelligence for Law Firms* published in November 2012, by The ARK Group. Zena is a sessional instructor at the University of Toronto iSchool, recently served as the Chair SLA Competitive Intelligence Division Board of Directors, and is a former member of the SCIP Board of Directors. She can be reached at @ZAppleCI.

Jeffrey Asjes works as a research and reference attorney at Fastcase, an online legal publishing company based in Washington, DC. His work focuses on the application of data analytics to legal issues, with the goal of automating simple but labor intensive tasks, such as proper citation formatting or recognizing subsequent negative treatment of cases. Prior to starting at Fastcase, Jeffrey worked on policy and outreach for the United Nations Information Center and the Partnership for a Secure America.

Born in Zurich, Switzerland, Jeffrey Asjes earned an A.B. from Princeton University and a J.D. from the Georgetown University Law Center, where he focused on the intersection of law and technology. At Georgetown, Jeffrey also worked for the Law Library's Faculty Services program; conducting legal research for Georgetown Law professors and streamlining the Library's information retrieval process.

Patrick Fuller is the vice president of business development for Neota Logic, Inc., based in New York City. With nearly 20 years of experience in the legal profession, Patrick is often referred to as one of the leading experts and pioneers in legal competitive intelligence (CI), particularly in the art of translating big data into intelligence for business development (BD) and organizational strategy purposes. Previously, Patrick served as the director of legal analytics for TyMetrix and ELM Solutions, helping legal departments to design and implement analytics and metrics management strategies. Prior to joining TyMetrix, he served as the vice president of product & market strategy for legal technology company Content Pilot. Additionally, Patrick was a senior consultant in the Client Growth Strategy practice with LawVision Group as well as an adjunct consultant with Hildebrandt Consulting, after serving as the global managing director of the Monitor Suite competitive intelligence platform he helped launch for Thomson Reuters Hubbard One. Patrick began his career in the legal industry with Martindale-Hubbell.

Mark Gediman is the director of information services for Best Best & Krieger, LLP and has been with BB&K since 2000, managing the research needs of more than 200 attorneys and paralegals in nine offices from DC to California. He is a past-president of the Southern California Association of Law Libraries (SCALL) and the co-founder and co-chair of the Competitive Intelligence Caucus of the Private Law Libraries-Information Professionals (PLL-IP) of the American Association of Law Libraries (AALL). He has over 25 years of experience in law library management and writes regularly on Competitive Intelligence, research, and library management issues. He presents frequently for AALL and the Inland Counties Association of Paralegals as well as for SCALL, NoCALL, ACI and HALL. He has authored Chapter 8 of *Business Intelligence for Law Firms* (ARK Group, 2012) and articles in *AALL Spectrum*, *Practicing Law Management Week*, *Paralegal Today*, and *Facts & Findings* – The Magazine of the National Assoc. of Legal Assistants (NALA). He is a graduate of the University of California, Riverside.

Joanna Goodman is a freelance journalist and writer based in London covering business and technology topics for national publications. She is the IT columnist for the *Law Society Gazette* and writes regular features for the *Guardian* about cutting-edge technology developments including artificial intelligence, virtual assistants, and virtual and augmented reality. Joanna has written several short films and an independent feature film, *Alfheim's Edge* (2016). She is the author of *Robots in Law* published by ARK Group in 2016. She has an MBA in strategic management from Kingston University. She likes technology, dance classes and travelling to new destinations.

Annie Johnson is the manager of business intelligence for Pillsbury Winthrop Shaw Pittman. At Pillsbury, Annie is responsible for maintaining and growing the firm's business intelligence structure.

Prior to joining Pillsbury, Annie spent nearly a decade covering business and public policy on the local, state, and national levels for various news organizations. At the *Nashville Business Journal*, where she covered economic development and legal affairs, Annie was instrumental in spurring public debate about tax-payer money and corporate incentives.

Previously a congressional reporter in Washington DC, Annie reported on the intricacies of the legislative and budgetary process. A native of Virginia, Annie also worked at various news outlets including the *Charlottesville Daily Progress*, *The Roanoke Times*, and the *Blue Ridge Business Journal*. In Roanoke, she was a weekly guest on an NPR affiliate where she hosted *Business Talk with Annie*.

In 2007, Annie was a stringer for *Time* magazine during the Virginia Tech shootings. She is a magna cum laude graduate of Randolph-Macon Woman's College in Lynchburg, VA, where she holds a bachelor's degree in economics.

Mark Medice is responsible for strategic marketing and new program development at Intapp, helping law firms to achieve client success using metrics and actions, exploring innovation in client service.

Prior to Intapp, Mark led the Peer Monitor program at Thomson Reuters, consulting with law firm leaders on topics like financial competitive intelligence and benchmarking, industry performance, rates, pricing trends and strategy, profitability, among other metrics. He is a licensed attorney and also worked throughout his career with Morgan Lewis, IBM, and Procter & Gamble.

Peter Lane Secor is the director of strategic pricing and project management with Pepper Hamilton LLP. Mr Secor concentrates on legal project management with a focus on improving efficiencies through shared management responsibilities, strengthening communication and making value transparent. His expertise includes client/matter profit analysis and providing partners with performance evaluations from a financial perspective.

Jennifer Roberts is responsible for the analytics and research component that supports thought leadership and new initiatives at Intapp. She examines the legal industry to drive analytical intelligence that informs strategic decisions and solves organizational needs.

Prior to joining Intapp, Jennifer was responsible for the innovation and development of thought leadership content at Thomson Reuters. Working with law firms to develop insightful and actionable content as well as working internally to educate the field. Jennifer received her master's degree from the Humphrey School of Public Policy, focusing on statistical methodology and performance measures within various industries. Jennifer can be reached at Jennifer.Roberts@Intapp.com.

Ed Walters is the CEO of Fastcase, a legal publishing company based in Washington, D.C. Fastcase is one of the world's largest legal publishers, serving more than 800,000 subscribers from around the world. He is an adjunct professor at the Georgetown University Law Center, where he teaches The Law of Robots, a class about the frontiers of law and technology.

Before founding Fastcase, Ed worked at Covington & Burling, in Washington D.C. and Brussels, where he advised Microsoft, Merck, SmithKline, the Business Software Alliance, the National Football League, and the National Hockey League. His practice focused on corporate advisory work for software companies and sports leagues, and intellectual property litigation.

Ed worked in the White House from 1991–1993, first in the Office of Media Affairs and then in the Office of Presidential Speechwriting. He has written for the *Washington Post*, the *New York Times*, *The University of Chicago Law Review*, *The Green Bag*, and *The Legal Times*.

Ed earned an A.B. in government from Georgetown University and a J.D. from the University of Chicago. He served as an editor of *The University of Chicago Law Review*. From 1996-97, he served as a judicial clerk with the Hon. Emilio M. Garza on the US Court of Appeals for the Fifth Circuit. He is a member of the American Bar Association, the Virginia State Bar, and the District of Columbia Bar.

Chapter 1:
Client success through better intelligence

By Mark Medice, senior director, and Jennifer Roberts, senior analyst at Intapp Client Success

"The purpose of business is to create and keep a customer"
Peter Drucker

We are living in a time of dramatic innovation, creating transformative business opportunities and risks. Many technological advances are arriving at such a rapid pace that they are creating varying degrees of excitement, acceptance, and for some anxiety. Lawyers have traditionally been resistors to these changes due in part to personality traits that make up a great lawyer. These are characteristics that drive success in legal practice, but can also lead to caution and increased scrutiny with new ideas. It is a lawyer's job to spot risk, and change is inherently risky, so it is natural to resist.[1] In spite of its benefits, however, this skepticism has held the legal profession back when it comes to client service.

In today's legal marketplace, it is no longer enough to be a great lawyer. Rather, a holistic approach is required, where a firm builds integrated service teams around the practice. Today, the opportunity to utilize modern intelligence technologies to systematize differentiated service strategies presents a compelling argument for what we call "client success".

Client success is a broad term that describes methods and practices to help firms realize their client potential. These initiatives rely on client intelligence systems to take advantage of digital data to offer insights, facilitate collaboration, and offer guided action in these endeavors.

Outside the legal industry, 78 percent of businesses are using client experience and design as a market differentiator.[2] Service design has shown to decrease operating costs and increase revenue through reducing client attrition, building stronger relationships, and winning new business.[3] According to Forrester Research, hotel chains have reaped the biggest benefit of deploying customer success initiatives, gaining $1.364 billion of revenue. A majority of that ($825 billion) is attributed to retaining business that might otherwise have been lost to competitors. Additionally, hotels with above average client experience have the potential to earn a cumulative $495 million in revenue from additional purchases.[4] The most important aspect of this for a firm is focusing on the client as a means to retain and attract new business from existing clients.

Client centricity is not a new phenomenon for law firms. However, applying a holistic approach that calls for the firm to act as one remains aspirational for most. Thus, this chapter strives to explore techniques to move firms towards service differentiation through client intelligence.

State of the industry

As noted above, due to lawyer psyche, there is a general tendency on the part of lawyers to embrace new ideas slowly, but it is worth briefly illustrating the consequences of this attitude. For example, in the area software adoption, law firms held on to the use of outdated Wordperfect software for document processing through the 1980s. They were very late in the use of email systems and of the internet in the 1990s, and in recent years have achieved marginal success rates in deploying customer relationship management (CRM) and client service systems.[5]

But these phenomena do not just apply to technology change. Firms have been slow to adopt management changes as well, such as creating diverse leadership teams and partnership ranks,[6] promoting women,[7] modifying compensation models to better motivate partners towards the greater whole,[8] as well as holding onto inefficient business practices such as billing by the hour.[9]

Other forces slowing adoption include the traditional partnership management model, which creates a leadership-by-chaos environment, where real change is attempted via an uphill battle to achieve consensus, and consequently few major initiatives are completed. There are also generational issues such as succession, where a large number of partners are within a decade or so of retirement, possessive of client relationships, and not as inclined to embrace new ideas.

Firms should take heed. If they can make a difference in any number of these areas, big gains may be realized in their brand, service, and law practice overall, thus differentiating the firm from competitors.

Client intelligence opportunity

The world is full of data today, big data. The very best and brightest companies are leveraging this data and turning it into competitive intelligence, affording them a leg up on the competition as they allow big data to teach them about their products, customers, and marketplace to attract, retain, and grow business. Think of Amazon, suggesting products based on what you have looked at and purchased and offering a community of reviewers. It is all about utilizing data to drive decisions.

Lawyers are fantastic data analysts. The essence of the legal practice consists of capturing data, analyzing it, and persuasively negotiating their way towards a positive client outcome. It follows logically then that the data-intensive world in which we live is ideal for the skills, instincts, and the daily routine of lawyers. If deployed properly, there is tremendous upside potential for the practicing lawyer and their firms.

The following section outlines three areas that might be explored in helping lawyers more effectively utilize data to maximize their client relationships, and along the way build stronger teams, using client intelligence systems. These areas are:

1. Understanding the power of systematic approaches;
2. Using new measurement systems made possible by modern technologies and pervasive data to align with new standards of performance expected by the client; and
3. Factoring in the cultural elements for introducing change, building on small wins, and sustaining a longer-range vision.

Before diving in, it is worth noting that when one considers the use of data as a prompt for organizational change, data can most effectively be applied if it answers a purpose. The stronger the mission accepted by the organization, the longer-lasting the change may be, and the new routines kept.

Data-driven and systematic approaches

The benefits of systematic approaches to process automation and data are well documented.[10] Common frameworks traditionally follow a progression from an immature, ad-hoc state of operation, to one that becomes more mature, smarter, measured, and proactive. Experts typically will also observe a degree of predictability and repeatability at later stages of maturity. This leads to a discussion of a maturity curve, and often is described analogously to a lifecycle, with the exception that unlike most lives, it is possible to regress to earlier stages of maturity if an organization retreats from the principles and practices that enabled its elevated state of performance. Therefore it requires continuous maintenance. Over time, the need to raise performance standards is required as new techniques and methods become available and known to the industry.

Using the maturity lifecycle model as a backdrop to competitive intelligence and firm client success strategy, we might assess not only where the industry is operating, but what the effort and hurdles might be as one advances to a higher level of performance. These efforts are going to face resistance, so the return on investment must be palpable. As outlined earlier in this chapter, the return on investment can be lofty, yielding top line revenue growth and also reduced costs through greater efficiency. Looking to systematize client interactions is unquestionably like going into the lion's den; it is quite a bit different than automating a manufacturing production line, which itself is no easy feat. By intervening in the service model, we are crossing into a realm of human judgment, which is tricky. We really don't know the steps to human thinking, because in spite of all our progress in scientific discovery, the brain largely remains a black box.

Take, for example, the motion of assessing a client situation, and answering a swathe of questions related to the overall relationship, such as:

- Is the client happy with our service?
- Are we a preferred provider?
- Do we know our client's business?
- Can we anticipate our client's needs?
- What pressures are our clients facing?
- How do our clients measure success?
- How do we measure success with our client?
- Are we meeting all our client's needs thoroughly?
- How does the client view our firm collectively?
- How does the client view the individual lawyers involved?
- Would the client refer us to others?

- Are we at risk of losing the client or being demoted in relative standing compared to other firms?
- Has our standing with the client improved or declined over the past year? and
- Are there aggregate patterns of risk or opportunity that might suggest actions on the part of the firm for the client portfolio?

Consider the situation of deploying an intelligence system to automate the answers to the questions above. One of the inherent cultural conflicts that frequently surfaces in these situations is the debate surrounding objective fact processing with human judgment. Can a system do better than a human at answering these questions and fulfilling these tasks? This is a false choice, as they will work most effectively together. The better perspective explores the strengths of each, enhancing the human decision-making process with an underlying support system. It is forewarned that this can be a culturally daunting task, but the firms that succeed at this will be stronger and more effective with their clients. This is an opportunity for sustained differentiation.

As an example, imagine a relationship partner who may feel very passionate about the nature of a client relationship, and be outright hostile to a complementary client data analysis of the situation. The partner may be spot on with their client assessment, but it may not be well communicated to team members, and the assessment may not be utilized in a way that provides for a unified client approach, resulting in fewer practices serving the client. Moreover, our research has informed us that frequently client assessments are not accurate, which results in unpleasant surprises when new business shifts elsewhere. This situation wreaks further havoc when partners leave or retire.

Looking at this in terms of the maturity lifecycle, it is imperative to assess where the organization is in terms of readiness to embrace system insights to support client questions. It is not an option to stand idle, but it is more than fair to acknowledge that law firms are relatively young in terms of traditional client service process maturity, and to factor that into the project plan. In spite of much discussion about the importance of client service and differentiation – and the true passion that most lawyers feel about serving their clients zealously – at the total firm level, there remains much work to do.[11]

These issues illustrate the importance of developing a framework and approach so that many of these measures and uses of data can take into account the human element, and provide the best chance of adoption and success. We will return to the cultural questions later in this chapter, but first we will discuss a client success measurement framework that builds on common law firm industry metrics.

Measurement, insights, and action

It is a generally accepted idea that measurement without a corresponding respondent action is substantially less potent, and ultimately of marginal value to any organization overall.[12] Thus any minimal data model in our view must contain at its core an insight accompanied by action, or said another way, data with meaning. One of the first things to consider in the context of a measurement framework is the core question of purpose and focus. Depending on the firm's aspirations, there may be desires to track performance, predict client opportunities, understand client risks, assist in the feedback loop to redesign the client experience, among many other goals that have both tactical and long-range aspirations. Measures should also take into account their context; for example, understanding whether it offers leading or predictive qualities (e.g. we are ranked as a preferred provider for 8 out of 10 of our key accounts, which forecasts that our revenue will grow by 20 percent over the next year), or whether it is a lagging or outcome-based measure (e.g. we achieved a realization rate of 75 percent and our profits per partner this year were $500,000). An action element is beneficial to facilitate an appropriate response, aiding stakeholders to join together to address issues and opportunities.

As we explore a sample framework for client success measurement and action, we will return to the maturity model to suggest that while most firms will benefit from a set of measures, each firm will likely need to match the portfolio of metrics and actions with the firm's overall readiness for adoption, strategy, and cultural preference. The key is to be thoughtful about getting started, and gaining traction while building out a larger vision. One size will not fit all for deployment, but it is worth remembering that the final arbiter of the firm's success is the client, who will have little patience or concern for a law firm's culture. Be on guard of the interloper who steals your client while you ponder culture. Lag at your own risk.

The tables below are designed to illustrate a portfolio of metrics that can be combined to answer key client questions. The first example illustrates client relationship health, and the second, client development and growth.

Measure	Description	Source
Client sentiment	Client feelings, perceptions, and experiences with the firm that reach a conclusion.	Client interviews, post-matter pulse checks, latent measurements like payment indicators, premium services, rates, profitability.
Practice penetration	Number of practices serving the client.	Fees billed to the firm at some level of materiality.
Wallet share	Percentage of business earned by the law firm from the total addressable client spend.	This is critically important and very difficult to measure. Firms might use proxies or estimates to produce this.
Matter velocity	New work received.	Review of new matter intake weighted by budget.
Acuity	Value of work relative to firm strategic position.	Fee-weighted classification of work.
Relationship depth	Examination of breadth and depth of relationships from the client and firm.	Review communications, expense reports, time entries, time and billing as well as other systems of record.
Financial performance/ Terms	Are the terms fair and mutually beneficial or is the relationship one-sided.	Review outside counsel guidelines, rate structure, realization rates, client profitability.

Table 1: Relationship health

Measure	Description	Source
Client sentiment	Client feelings, perceptions, and experiences with the firm that reach a conclusion.	Client interviews, post-matter pulse checks, latent measurements like payment indicators, premium services, rates, profitability.
Referrals	Client and partner referrals.	Referrals weighted by fees by clients and internally by partners.
Relationship indexing	Traversing relationships to identify new client opportunities.	Review matter intake, communications, expense reports, time entries, time and billing, and other systems of record.
Client industry	Client industry.	Client entity name match to NAICS code.
Practice referrals	Reference table by matter type that suggests opportunities for work based on work being performed by the firm and client.	Reference table by matter type.
Practice penetration	Number of practices serving the client.	Fees billed to the firm at some level of materiality.
Client situation	Client needs for our services, today and forward-looking.	Client information, news, regulatory changes, objectives, goals.
Collaboration/ Engagement	Collaborative and engagement towards the greater good that the partners and other professionals possess.	A mix of referrals, cross-practice work on matters, new ideas/ innovations, attrition, engagement surveys, among others.

Table 2: Client growth measurement

Some of the measures above can be directly calculated from existing data, while others might require proxies or human input. The key is not to build out a dictionary of measurement indicators that leave the firm awash with data (i.e. more is not better), but to suggest a number of ways to systematically understand performance. Start with a smaller group of measures with simple actions and observe their efficacy against questions they are addressing. The measures should be created in a context that takes into account the various roles and responsibilities in the firm, and offers some guidance as to the appropriate response, even if the action is modest.

Cultural considerations

Change is hard for everyone. Lawyer change is even harder. However, against all odds, firms must overcome these hurdles to enhance the client experience. Other industries can act as a guiding light for law firms where the concept of client experience is already well established. Successful models that already exist are driven by companies like Delta, American Express, and Sprint. Leadership is the strongest element present within these models. In fact, these companies are making room at the executive management level, appointing chief client officers and chief experience officers to own customer success and drive client intelligence in a systematic company-wide manner.[13] Other elements include a clear mission and vision, as well as the development of performance metrics driving accountability. In total, these programs provide structure to facilitate education, compliance, and foster innovation. As these companies can attest, if done well, the benefits can be returned in greater force and lead to meaningful market gains.

One of the difficulties in this kind of effort, however, is that while there may be common elements utilized, the strategy and priorities followed by one may not be suitable for its competitor. Copycats should be wary. This is an area that requires some homework and thought. When a professional service firm goes about the design of client service, it calls for reflection about the underlying principles and values of the firm.[14]

Managing progress in light of the larger vision

For every client intelligence project undertaken, there will be a mountain of objections and myriad reasons for delay. Whether it is by design or human nature, resistance should be expected and tactics to overcome it should be built into the plan. Based on our research, a top-down, paint-the-vision motion, combined with a bottom-up, gain momentum strategy will be sufficient to carry out the plan. Find practices or sub-practices, offices, or other logical combinations of the firm who embrace the larger vision, and are willing to give it practical application. Perhaps their success will garner attention and envy towards a larger movement.

Note that we are not suggesting taking shortcuts against bona fide issues that must be thought through carefully; for example, managing client confidences and preserving trusted relationships. We are also not suggesting using a competitive intelligence system to sully the reputation of partners or other professionals in the firm. The idea is to use the newly available intelligence to make the firm smarter. Nothing will stifle the progress of a data-centric initiative faster than having the members observe its use as means of individual destruction.

Summary

Leadership expert John Maxwell once said: "Change is inevitable but growth is optional." The use of client intelligence systems will provide a part of the answer to bring law firms closer to their clients, fostering growth and differentiation. The model outlined throughout this chapter aspires to move firms towards a unified client vision, better informing firm stakeholders about actions that they might not naturally perform, and coordinating these activities to enable teamwork and collaboration. Ideally, the systems deployed could offer some level of predictive value that will enable a much stronger capability for the firm in anticipating client needs, improving communications during the matter, and executing service and support. Change may be inevitable, but today it provides a special opportunity for firms to succeed. For those who can break through the resistance, the rewards are significant.

References

1. Dr Larry Richards' work on the personality profile of lawyers and psychological dimensions like resiliency and risk can be found on lawyerbrain.com.
2. Econsultancy, "Quarterly Digital Intelligence Briefing: 2015 Digital Trends", January, 2015.
3. See: https://econsultancy.com/reports/quarterly-digital-intelligence-briefing-2015-digital-trends/https://econsultancy.com/reports/quarterly-digital-intelligence-briefing-2015-digital-trends/.
4. Manning, H., & Bodine, K. *Outside In*, New Harvest Books, New York, 2012.
5. Ibid.

6. Keeping in mind that CRM systems and their roots go back at least 30 years in terms of deployment in other industries.
7. "The Inclusive Workplace: Legal Laggards Begin to Master Diversity Briefs", *Financial Times*, March, 2014. See: www.ft.com/intl/cms/s/0/a9a70d38-d522-11e3-9187-00144feabdc0.html#axzz3wQMAHVZr.
8. American Bar Association, "A Current Glance at Women in the Law", July, 2014. See: www.americanbar.org/content/dam/aba/marketing/women/current_glance_statistics_july2014.authcheckdam.pdf
9. Gardner, H.K., "When Senior Managers Won't Collaborate", *Harvard Business Review*, March, 2015.
10. Not just as a billing unit, but also a bonus unit.
11. Soliditech, "7 Benefits of Business Process Automation", January, 2014. See: blog.soliditech.com/blog/7-benefits-of-business-process-automation.
12. Mark Medice recently moderated a panel of general counsel, asking what law firms should do more of, to which all three respondents stated more frequent checkpoints and conversations about their needs. In spite of common industry discussion about client interviews and checkpoints, law firm activity in this area remains very infrequent and ad-hoc.
13. Even if this idea occasionally gets overlooked in the heat of the moment or due to the sizzle of the visual presentation.
14. Hagen, P., "The Rise of the Chief Customer Officer", *Harvard Business Review*, 18 April 2011. See: hbr.org/2011/04/the-rise-of-the-chief-customer.
15. Sinek, S. *Start With Why: How Great Leaders Inspire Everyone to Take Action*, Portfolio Penguin, London, 2009.

Chapter 2: Why client intelligence is (or should be) the new CI for law firms

By Zena Applebaum, director of competitive intelligence at Bennett Jones LLP

They say the only constant is change and for more than the past decade, during which I have been working in the field of CI for law firms, neither CI nor law firms have been immune to change. Both have gone through a period of great transition – transitions that are not yet complete and will likely continue to evolve over the course of at least another decade. Then of course, as nature would have it, it will all change again.

I strongly believe that now more than ever there is a need for robust CI capabilities in law firms. But I think we need to rethink exactly how we define "CI". The CI that law firms really need to consider, and which I will be referring to in this chapter is *client* intelligence. This CI may look and feel very different from the CI you are used to reading about in text books, but the fundamentals are still there:

1. Define key intelligence topics and questions (what surprises do we want to avoid?);
2. Find research sources and elicit information from primary, secondary, and HUMINT sources;
3. Analyze the intelligence you have gathered using one or more analysis techniques (hat tip to Bensoussan and Fleisher[1]);
4. Disseminate your intelligence throughout the firm in a format that is useful and *actionable*; and
5. Repeat.

The CI cycle

Traditional competitive intelligence is about cutting through the vast amounts of clutter or data using analytical methods to produce insights and drive business decisions. Whether we are talking about structured (quantitative) or unstructured (qualitative) data, the role of the

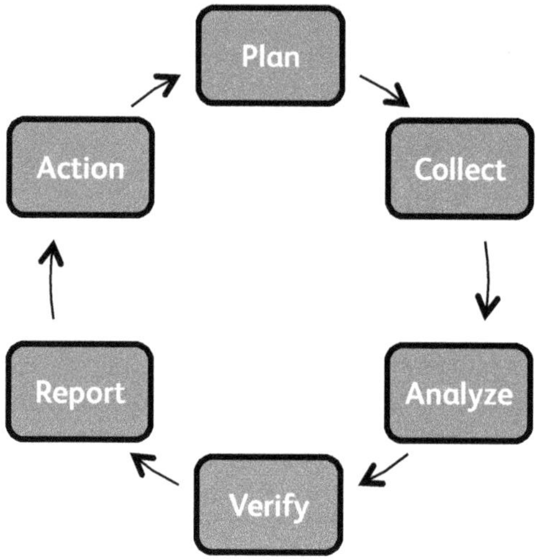

Figure 1: The CI cycle

intelligence practitioner is to help a firm avoid surprises, make actionable recommendations, and inform decision making. But still, I would argue, there is more – there has always been something more – to legal CI. Something that sets legal CI apart, something that may well be a part of other industry CI functions; but from what I have seen, read, and experienced of late, should be the cornerstone of legal CI. This is something that I have been unknowingly practicing for years, but have only recently begun to articulate. Legal CI is *client intelligence*, or CRM-plus.

And then it was 2008 – An industry in flux

Quite simply, the legal market has significantly changed in the last several years. The effects have been incremental in some cases, as with growing internal departments or a focus on alternative billing, but in all cases, the changes can be attributed to the perfect coming together of three factors, as illustrated in Figure 2.

Writing this in early 2016, for the first time in recent history, law firm clients are in the driving seat when it comes to legal purchasing decisions, preferred pricing, and general efficiency of firms. In the past, given the highly specialized services that lawyers had to offer, firms could price those services as they wished and clients had few or no alternatives. If a client needed litigation, or advice and the related documentation to do a deal, they were forced to pay what law firms commanded. In

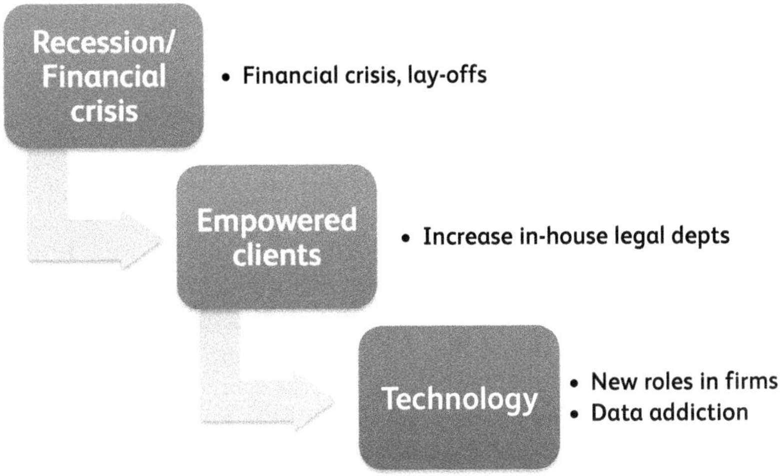

Figure 2: Factors driving change in the legal industry

the last several years, especially since 2008, the competitive climate has changed. Legal services are no longer the domain of the law firm. It is really that simple. Competition and consolidation have increased, alternative legal firms have emerged, clients have options, and more importantly they have found their voices.

Once upon a time, firms could send a bill to clients with not a single itemized item, just a list of lawyers and hours, and the client would have no recourse but to pay the bill. Overtime, disbursements and matter times were added to the bills, but the hourly rate remained an unquestioned standard of the practice and business of law. Then, 2008 happened, and the demand for high-priced legal services tumbled in the recession. The capacity law firms had added over the years to meet the robust demand and maintain their profitable leverage was no longer necessary, yet firms still had massive overheads as a result of the padded associate ranks, high rents in major urban centered towers, and all manner of spending in between. Feeling and seeing the waste post-recession, clients (somewhat en masse) decided to start putting pressure on firms to provide commoditized services – at more reasonable rates, to provide alternatives to the hourly rate – and volume discounts were not the answer. The term "value" entered the client lexicon for the first time in a very real and tangible way, and clients demanded value for their money. To add to the pressure on firms, corporations were consolidating and slimming their ranks too, post 2008, and procurement departments started to get involved in the purchasing decisions for law firms. The cronyism approach to file referrals was under siege in favor of more transparency, more requests for proposal (RFP), vendor of record panels, and preferred provider lists. Companies started to look at consolidating the number of external counsel, asking for automation of routine tasks, and generally applying any number of cost pressures to firms.

At the same time, firms burdened with high overheads were letting people go, the "Lay Off List" of 2008/2009 was, for a period of time, the most frequently read column with the morning's coffee. The irony, of course, is that many of those who were laid off went in-house, building in-house departments that not only rival some small firms in terms of head count, but are able to perform much of the same work they did as external counsel at a fraction of the cost to the company. These law firm expats are well positioned to know where firms can trim their bills, increase efficiency, and provide additional services to corporate counsel. Today, there are all kinds of alternatives as well, from outsourcing firms to "lawyer on demand" contract services, and process automation. There is to-the-minute e-billing, and firms have pushed many ancillary functions outside of the high-rent urban centers.

The legal market has become a "buyer's market", and if market research has taught the western world anything, it is that buyers can be swayed. However, we need to get to know our buyers, their habits, their likes and dislikes, and most importantly their needs and their pain points. This is client intelligence.

Technology makes it easy

Technology, its accessibility, and our modern addiction to data has turned everyone into an intelligence broker of some kind. "Intelligence" as a term is popping up everywhere from "emotional intelligence" to "social media intelligence". Net Promoter scores and Twitter Clout scores come up in everyday conversations as well as other topics formerly reserved for the computer science degreed only, like analytics, metrics, and data visualizations. Some of the data hype is opportunistic and serves to do little else than market products, rather than providing any meaningful benefit. But some of the data analytics and intelligence does have legs. Information is changing at a rapid pace, from photographs that are shared and deleted in seconds, to databases that warehouse the minutia details of deals or that parse legal agreements into its composite parts, and someone is expected or needed to make sense of it all.

In many firms, the person or group charged with "making sense of it all" is the CI person. But, it does not necessarily have to fall to CI. Given the influx of data, there are many new roles established to help with data discovery; there are data scientists and business intelligence professionals that would argue that this is their domain, and they would each be right. The point is that no longer is there a clear "owner" of information or intelligence in the general corporate community or in law firms. Law firms in particular, being organizations whose currency rests in the ability to produce, distill, and manipulate words on a page, understand that there is power in information. And law firms also have the benefit or the challenge of having individuals tasked with knowledge management, library services, business research, client analytics, and all sorts of other data centers. Where law firms fall victim to their siloed innovation is in not knowing how to connect all the various data centers in a profitable and smart way.

Firms are trying to make sense of it all and we have started to see a whole new crop of law firm management and administration types as a result of these new pressures on firms. Roles like pricing directors, knowledge managers, Six Sigma Law Firm leaders, directors of innovation, legal project managers, client officers, sales people, and even data scientists – this latest crop of new law firm titles and roles beautifully illustrates the changing environment within firms and the reluctant or (in some cases enthusiastic) acceptance that the models of yesterday are no longer working. Firms needed to change the way they bill, the way they practice, and ultimately the way they market.

Clients have changed, aided and abetted by technology, and as a result the buyers of legal services are far more sophisticated than they were, even a decade ago. Add sophistication to the new found voice of the client and again you can begin to understand how the legal market has changed, forever.

Understand my business

Clients have access to a large proportion of the same data as you do, which means that clients know what firms know. The informational playing field has been leveled. Information – access to it and use of it alone is not a competitive advantage. Today, clients expect that you will know their legal spend, you'll know what their greatest business challenges and weaknesses are, and they likely have someone doing CI on their end keeping them informed about how the market is changing and helping them to change along the way too. The opportunity for CI in this space is to share what you know, that the client doesn't know that you know, such as their lead competitors, their regulatory and business issues and their current marketing campaigns, even highlights of their twitter feeds. That magical "thing" that will allow you to provide better service, to stand out from the crowd, and the element that demonstrates that you know and understand the client's business.

As Acritas – Sharp Legal, BTI, or any other syndicated research or survey of law firm clients will tell you, law firms are not chosen based on price. RFPs, and client work generally, is yours to lose or win based on how well you know the client. This is where the elusive value proposition of firms is demonstrated, and where typical ongoing CI products such as daily briefs, newsletters, and dossiers really come into play. CI cannot be about being informed "just in time" with a taxi pack or dossier anymore, but about being up-to-date with your client as an ongoing concern and a matter of differentiation and firm survival. Being a trusted business advisor is not about providing tax advice once a year as a 10-K gets filed, but about keeping your client informed all year, all the time, about their business's exposure, risk, and market. CI can help bridge the gap between client expectations and attorney knowledge on an ongoing, consistent basis. This is where firms become accountable not just to the dollar figures which are increasingly scrutinized, but also to business issues and the ability to provide more for less. I liken this new response to clients to "CRM-plus". Relationships with clients today cannot be maintained purely through providing good legal service at reasonable rates. Dr Sylvia Hodges Silverstien, writing on "The Evolution of Legal Consumers" in Forbes magazine in 2014 describes the new client/attorney relationship in this way as well: "...law firms should no longer rely on building relationships, but have to be able to also argue with numbers, proving that working with them also makes good business sense".

To put this discussion into tangible terms, let's do a "then competitive intelligence" vs a "now client intelligence" comparison of a simple and typical activity – responding to an RFP.

RFP support then

RFP support is how I fell into CI while working at Canada's then-largest law firm, circa 2003. We were asked to bid on a piece of work to bring a major US retailer to Canada. I was responsible for putting the firm's response together, and in addition to knowing who else would be putting forward a bid and what their teams might look like, I wanted to add some intelligence and influence to this proposal. I knew the retailer would be a success in Canada and that it would be a great piece of work for my firm and the multiple practices that the support of such a client would require.

Back then, I would have researched not just who is the incumbent firm on a particular piece of business, but who else is working in the space, how does the prospect present itself and how can my bid team match and mirror the prospect's language, diversity expectations (which wasn't even really a thing yet, but I could see it was coming), corporate culture, and the like. Depending on the prospect and the nature of the RFP, we would canvass others who have worked with the prospect or who have relationships there – get a human intelligence angle on the prospect to inform our bid or even just to know what we know and file it away for use at a second interview. The process was easy and straightforward, but important. It relied largely on secondary intelligence with a sprinkle of primary intelligence and would fit nicely into a SWOT or other simple framework.

RFP support now

Today, I would do all the things I would have done in the past, only as a result of an ongoing CI program. I have dashboards set up for each client of interest that aggregates internal data as well as external news reports and analysis about the client or prospect. I can set these up on the fly as well and monitor a client or prospect during the RFP response window. So, I can assess the client or prospect daily and "get to know" their business and other issues.

At the same time, I would add elements of data analytics to my research and CI analysis, meaning I would combine the qualitative and unstructured data from the news with quantitative data about the prospect's spend with our firm in the past, or its market cap. I would also spend time understanding and getting to know the prospect over social media. I would have the advantage of robust data sets – neatly provided by third parties or exported and manipulated into the CSV myself, like previous billing info, legal spend on previous transactions, and all kinds of other data sets that are now at my fingertips to plot on graphs, add to analysis frameworks, and devise a plan for winning the work.

I would also go into the RFP armed with my firm's own win/loss analysis, from which I would know why we typically win or lose work in a sector, with this type of client or that, which preferred billing rates or AFAs are more likely to win the work, and how weather patterns may affect our firm's chances of winning work. I jest on that last point, but in effect, we have become far more sophisticated in our approach to answering even the simplest of client questions like: "Why should we give your firm our work?" The truth is, today, even that question (the very basis for the RFP) has changed considerably to something more like: "Can you prove that you are the most efficient firm to meet our legal and pricing needs and that you will provide exceptional value in addition to the highest level of legal expertise?"

Firms are looking at ways to generate the data they need to satisfy the data hunger of clients, but law firms are set up with the intention of practicing law not collecting, or more importantly understanding, data. For me, this along with technology mentioned earlier, is the strongest opportunity for CI people in law firms. CI in firms has the unique advantage of being able to "speak" the languages and dialects of everyone else in the firm. That is to say, a good CI practitioner should be able to flow seamlessly between the qualitative and the quantitative. As new roles are created in firms, CI should be the bridge that connects the internal data of the accounting departments, the "pricing people", the "Six Sigma Belted people", with the external data, current awareness, or news content of the "marketing people", the librarians, and the CI folks themselves.

Client intelligence has the capacity to act as the collaborator and disseminator between the various groups, and with those in management and practice. I am a huge fan of internal firm collaboration; I strongly believe that administrative and management groups working better together in law firms is a massive differentiator for firms. It is not something you can explain to clients, but the efforts and the output will be recognized and appreciated by clients. When those of us tasked with supporting attorneys work well together, the firm can be more client focused, more driven, and more successful. Of course, that's no easy feat. There are all sorts of reasons not to work well together; traditionally the departments have been siloed and firms have done well (commercially) so why change? Making an effort to collaborate and break silos, as trite as it sounds, can help firms define their cultural DNA and understand who they are in the market, and how their billing and client mix reflects this. CI can then build these discoveries through a series of tactical and strategic initiatives and programs that require little time or attention from lawyers who are busy billing clients.

Collaboration is the key to client intelligence

We know that clients want to work with firms who know their business. What does knowing a business mean? In the data-rich, technology-savvy, empowered client world today, it means understanding the client's market, their business issues, their liabilities, their risks, and their successes *as they happen*. Knowing the client is about having a grasp on the client's business that goes beyond the most recent press release issued or its website home page or how you responded to a recent RFP. Knowing a client is about making the client feel like you work at their place of business every day. "Business savvy" is a 25 percent driver of law firm recommendations from general counsels interviewed by Acritas in 2015. Furthermore, when general councils (GCs) were asked about what additional skills they would like to see the lawyers they work with on a day to day basis have additional training or development in, the top answer was "understanding the client's business". That, to me, is where CI comes into play (client intelligence, that is). The role of CI in law firms is to help lawyers understand their clients business so that the lawyers and firm as a whole can serve their clients in a proactive and advisory manner. Knowing the client's business – the successes, the failures, and everything in between – will be a reflection on the lawyer's business savvy and will then have a snowball effect that will impact a firm's own position and ability to be and stay competitive.

I am not suggesting that CI is the holy grail of law firm administration and management or BD, but I do think that – along with Legal Project Management (LPM) and other post-2008 technology-backed, data-centered initiatives – CI has a significant role to play, from strategic planning and key account programs, to informing BD tactics and differentiated marketing campaigns. CI is aimed at helping firms to avoid surprises by bringing a robust analysis and color to any firm initiative. A firm without client intelligence today would be a like a sportscast without the color: the score won't change, but the experience will be a little less impactful for everyone involved.

Five steps to successful client intelligence

1. Know your client:
   - Differentiate from the competition by understanding your client; and
   - Listen and learn from client feedback;

2. Be tenacious, relentless in the pursuit of client service:
   - The only competitive advantage is client service, knowing your client. Know your client (on behalf of your attorneys);

3. Check your ego:
   - Be collaborative, break silos, and share information for intelligence success;

4. Harness technology:
   - Use access to technology as an opportunity to go beyond the tools; and

5. Evolve:
   - Get out and be seen, continue to grow your CI function and yourself.

Reference

1. Bensoussan, B.E. and Fleisher C.S., *Business and Competitive Analysis: Effective Application of new and Classic Methods*, 2nd edition, Pearson Education, New Jersey, 2015.

Chapter 3:
Balancing pricing and client perceptions of value

By Peter Lane-Secor, director of strategic pricing and project management at Pepper Hamilton LLP

"Price is what you pay. Value is what you get."
Warren Buffett

The word "value" is inherently complicated. Riddled with preconceived notions of "what we get" in exchange for "what we pay". Consider, value-based misperceptions predate us all; the well-known aphorism "beauty is in the eye of the beholder" first appeared in Greek philosophy circa 300 BC. More notably, the concept of value is *not unique* to legal. Yet many struggle with this simple five-letter concept because modern interpretations vary from individual to individual, profession to profession, and situation to situation.

Today, "value" could mean one thing to a law firm – and an entirely different thing to that firm's client. Creating "value harmony"– where firm and client (stakeholders) have a shared understanding of the value delivered for fees – requires listening and educating on the part of *both parties*. In this chapter, we will examine how to define value, potential results of not defining value at the outset, some methods of demonstrating value, and fee structures designed to mirror the value provided. This process, when done right, empowers wiser decision-making on both sides of the buy/sell exchange and transcends disputes over pricing.

Defining value

Clients hire law firms that they believe are capable of achieving a desired result. Arguably, this part is assumed. Value is delivered by outperforming the desired result and/or the manner in which it's delivered. "Knocking it out of the park" results may even result in a bonus. To deliver and demonstrate "knock it out of the park" results, firms must listen to and understand – in advance – the expectations of *all* stakeholders in the matter: the general counsel, executives, board members, business units, etc. More often than not, this entails educating the client stakeholders about both what to expect as the matter unfolds, and how the firm intends to approach the work. This working together shapes the definition of value for each situation. Consider that firms are hired for their expertise. These experts need to help clients understand their legal and business options. Read: the arbitrary distinction between the "practice of law" and "the business of law" is a primary part of the problem. But working together – beginning with the value-setting process – creates a shared management responsibility, so the best strategy can be customized for each unique situation. To do so, law firms must cultivate an ability to convey *the effort required* to accomplish the client's objectives.

Take the evolution of outside counsel guidelines (OGC), aka terms and conditions. Recall that the document's original intention had been to align outside counsel's representation with the client's legal strategy. Not to restrict every possible cost factor. One of the best OCGs I've encountered did not limit the number of days for deposition prep. In fact, it *insisted* on at least three days of preparation. The document went on to explain how much the client valued the preparation, and the better results it produced in litigation. Today, OCGs excessively focus on micro-managing matters, down to the task, to ensure billing is as low as possible; barely referencing would-be "out of the park" results for each and every client. To be clear, we're not blaming companies for this. OGC – circa 2015 – are the direct result of bad behavior on the part of some firms. Particularly, our failure to work with our clients in advance on setting a shared understanding of the level of effort a matter will require.

Consider another example of how "missing the value-defining opportunity" plays out poorly. A newly elected partner had been assigned responsibility of lead partner for a new client who had been hit with an import injunction. Read: the company would be unable to sell their product in the United States. And our client-relationship contact was *frantic*, quickly conveying to our young, newly-elected partner that they would be out of business if the injunction was not lifted quickly. The partner quickly assembled a team and quickly got to work. Two partners, one associate, and one paralegal worked 10–14 hours per day, over Fourth of July weekend. The injunction response was filed quickly and dismissed promptly thereafter. The client would be able to import its products again and the business was saved!

It is safe to assume that *any* client would be delighted with such a quick – and indisputably – quality result. Fees for such an impactful contribution to the business would be a non-issue. Perhaps even a bonus should be discussed. Sadly, these assumptions would all be false. What the firm did not understand was the *broader* financial constraints the company was already experiencing. Our one invoice chronicled, in detail, the holiday weekend work. Total dollars, again for *indisputable* quality work *and* service, was north of $200,000. To say, "the client was not happy" would be an understatement. The company's profit margins were so small that it would take an influx of capital to pay our invoice.

Cleary, we had not done a good job of understanding the context. Nor did we do our job to educate the client about the effort and cost required to obtain the desired result. This failure to develop a value understanding – (new) partner *not asking*, (new) client *not sharing*, emotions (cortisone and adrenaline respectively), and speed – is the crux of almost all disputes over the price of legal services. In this case, the client pointed out after that in the UK, cost budgeting is a requirement for all claims valued at £10 million or less. Cases now brought into the net included commercial disputes and property claims which were previously subject to exemptions to cost budgeting. Know, the client still retained us for additional work, and for the injunction matter we ended up charging a reduced fee, utilizing a payment plan. Read: stakeholder alignment was achieved after the event; however, expectations about the work and the fee should always be crystalized in advance.

Using communications to demonstrate value

So, what can firms do better to get to a shared value understanding with clients? One method is to use forecasting as a communications tool. The process was originally developed jointly while working with a client's controller of legal services. The firm was constantly missing accrual budget targets in a series of expensive government actions. The problem was that the prosecutors and judges, some in elected positions, constantly changed schedules for document productions, depositions, hearings, and other events.

The solution was to create regular communications or touch points to discuss potential changes that would impact the budget. This was my first legal project management governance opportunity. Together, the client and the firm developed an annual budget at the start of the year. Every month, the internal firm team, attorneys, and pricing specialist would meet and discuss any budget variances for the prior month,

month to date progress, and any potential adjustments to the forecast. The client team included their lead counsel, the GC, and the client's legal controller. Each litigation team provided a couple of paragraphs on matter status and any requested forecast changes. This provided good ongoing documentation for the entire team, firm, and client. At the beginning, internal meetings and external in-person meetings were in excess of an hour. With time, meetings were reduced to 15 minutes per month, and in-person meeting converted to a phone call. Note: the forecasting process produced accurate spend estimates for millions of dollars per month. Ironically, the forecast variances were generally within thousands of dollars – often 1 percent or less of the total forecast.

Clearly, we solved for communication skills and more precise budgeting. But we also made progress on a long-existing struggle with aged accounts receivable balances, missed payments, and partial payments. The inventory back-log lifted and the client sent payments on a regular basis. Another notable benefit for the firm was a *40 percent plus increase in business with the client*. Note: this client had already been contributing tens of millions of dollars of annual revenue to the firm. For those looking to emulate similar results, let's consider why that revenue increased.

Establishing clear communication controls also means providing (additional?) opportunities to help the client: a) understand; and/or b) communicate *the value* the firm delivers with their own "non-lawyer" business units. For example, one business administrator was concerned about the hourly rate for discovery attorneys. The rate was about $45 per hour. The administrator asked if we could lower the rates. The firm had recently reduced the document production and review from 12 custodians for five years of data to three custodians, then subsequently to one custodian for three years. The savings were well in excess of $2 million. Consider the above business administrator in context. If we – the firm – had agreed to reduce the hourly rate by $10 – as per their request – it would have required *over 200,000 hours* to produce the same "value" the firm's pre-existing *effective and efficient* practices would deliver. The meetings provided an opportunity to explain this to the client. More notably, our opportunity to discuss would not have come if the administrator had not been included in the communications plan.

As aspiring law firm leaders, know our "quality" results will not translate well unless vehicles are created to share and explain them. Consider this the next time a case is dismissed early, or an early favorable settlement is achieved, or compliance plans and audits prevent a client from being hit with a massive class action or government investigation. The firm could very well have saved the client millions of dollars. Learn to become more proactive by helping in-house legal departments – and the business leaders they report to – to experience the value everyone provides to the business.

Estimates and fee structures

A critical part of demonstrating value is providing accurate fee estimates. There is a science and an art to everything. The "science" is what you do – the methods and the components. And to a degree, we should master them. The "art" is knowing when and how to use it. Attorneys first learning to budget or develop fee structures often *feel* that legal matters are too unpredictable to quantify. One client respectfully reminded a partner: "We build the impossible and tell our clients how much it will cost. How come you cannot do that with legal fees?" Helping attorneys to change their behavior – both internally and externally – is truly an art. Seasoned pricing professionals have learned which approach works best for each interaction. There is no "one size fits all" solution. The process begins with an ability to determine the factors driving the budget and fee estimate for each matter.

Developing an arsenal of approaches – historical run rates, hours/resources, componentized, phases, cost driver based, relational, and more – takes time and effort. Similarly, *people process information differently*. Professionals should be sensitive to these differences. Transcending miscommunication requires an ability to help each client understand the value received in exchange for the fees being charged. Consider developing an arsenal of approaches to present, explain, or customize the service-exchange "data" as well.

One simple and effective budgeting approach is to use historical run rates *aka analyze similar matters*. Gather historic matters. Look for: 1. who, 2. did what, and 3. when. Be sure to keep the "historic" nature of the work in context as new efficiencies and resource realignments are evolving quickly. That said, one issue both clients and firms encounter is how to identify "similar" matters.

A group of pricing and knowledge management professionals met at ILTACON in August 2015 and again at LawTech NY in February 2016 with the mission to develop a standard set of matter type codes. At Pepper Hamilton, we've had a standard matter taxonomy in place for years, as have many other firms. Note: applying matter codes consistently at intake (or shortly after) is also a part of the "identify similar" problem.

Whereever your organization falls on either spectrum of "capture and report on" capabilities, it is easy to manufacture a useful data set for each matter type. This begins with identifying cost drivers.

Pick an area of law. Gather the partners, associates, paralegals, and secretaries in a meeting. Ask everyone what drives the costs of a typical engagement. For example, litigation cost drivers typically include: jurisdiction, size of class, discovery size, knowledge of issue, level of contention, number and types of deponents, number and types of experts, length of trial, jury or bench, etc. Next, create a simple chart: one matter per row and cost driver columns. Finally, complete the chart together. Attorneys often remember most of the details, and most firms have systems that can help find the information. Even if the information is not 100 percent accurate, producing the list can be an invaluable resource. Now, a pricing analyst can begin to understand the relationships between the cost drivers.

Additional benefits of manufacturing a data set include:

a) facilitated learning experience for team;
b) a visual graphic/resource to help structure dialogue with clients about anticipated effort and results; which in turn
c) helps each client crystalize *their* value propositions.

Randy Steere, a legal software provider and developer, teaches that when first analyzing similar matters the "outliers" or matters with the biggest variance generally *teach us* the most. "What went wrong?" "Why was this resource used?" "Why was so much time spent on a particular task code?" Or, when analyzing a particular motion using narratives, "Why did one cost more than another?" Even if budgets do not change over the course of one engagement – which they often do – they certainly evolve with every new matter. Did we under – or over – quote the motion for summary judgment? If so, why? What were the drivers? Recall, *budgeting is a learning experience.* We get better every time we do one.

To understand the impact of cost drivers, we can pull run rate data for the various matters, effort by month, by timekeeper, and task code. If the plan is to rely exclusively on historic matter data, consider:

1) The delivery of legal service grows more efficient daily; and
2) Adjust the historic run rates to the current fee structure.

The next level of analysis is "analyzing narratives". This effort digs deeper into matter characteristics and produces insight to greatly assist with preparing accurate budgets. To be clear, plenty of technology solutions exist, capable of deriving insight from time narratives in a less manual/historic fashion. However, even without software or services, some good analysis can be done using Excel.

Export the data from the time entry system, dump time narratives into Excel, and then use the "search" function to find specific information. (Then buy a cool tech tool with pretty pictures and real-time insight so you don't have to do this – manually/historically – forever.)

Narrative	2015 STD	L530	Oral
Attend mock argument	$1,586	$1,586	
Review outline and Q/A	$396	$0	
Conference re oral argument preparation	$238	$238	$238
Attend argument	$1,427	$1,427	

=IFERROR(IF(SEARCH(AD$1,X48,1)>0,AB48,)",")

Table 1: Componentized budget

The results can be fascinating. One analysis of 15 depositions on various engagements produced a variance of only a few thousand dollars. From there, we were able to quote *accurately* what each type of deposition would cost. The same can be done for: motions, experts, diligence, and more. As your knowledge bank grows, projections can be adjusted based on primary (case variance) factors, e.g. level of contention. This "per-unit pricing" or "componentized pricing" helps everyone to truly understand costs, and aids in the discussion about where dollars are best spent to get the "biggest bang for your buck". In many cases, it's not the unit cost that drives the fee; *it is the number of units*. Take the budget example below. If we reduce plaintiff depositions to only $20,000, the overall cost of that deposition set is still $100,000. However, if we leave the per-unit price the same and reduce the deposition set from five to four, the overall cost drops to $90,000.

CASE

Budget and process

		Final		% Complete	
Initiative	**Unit fees**	**Units**	**Amount**	**%**	**Amount**
Analysis, strategy, communications, fact development, and investigation		X%	$150,000	22%	$33,000
Fact depositions					
Plaintiffs	$22,500	5	$112,500	20%	$22,500
Technicians	$14,000	3	$42,000	20%	$8,400
Attendants	$31,000	1	$31,000	20%	$6,200
CEO	$45,000	1	$45,000	20%	$9,000
Depositive motions					
Adequacy of the warning	$50,000	3	$150,000	25%	$37,500
Learned intermediary					
Other motions					
Motions based on facts of individual cases (plaintiff's knowledge)	$35,000	2	$70,000	40%	$28,000

Expert discovery					
Selection	$8,000	2	$16,000	100%	$16,000
Reports	$35,000	2	$70,000	50%	$35,000
Deposition	$21,000	2	$42,000	0%	$0
	$35,000				
Depose plaintiffs' experts	$18,000	2	$36,000	50%	$18,000
Settlement efforts					
Preparation days	$15,000	3	$45,000	33%	$14,850
Negotiation days	$20,000	2	$40,000	0%	$0

Table 2: Example budget

With this data, firms and clients can intelligently discuss the "who", "what", and "why" of a matter – preferably, at the outset. Doing so takes the value conversation to a new level. Why do we want to do this? What is the benefit? Is the desired result worth the price?

Once we've benchmarked the cost drivers, we can begin to understand the relationship between efforts. For example, the amount of discovery has a dramatic impact on the cost of a case. Using data, we can easily establish the dependency between discovery and overall case cost, or the cost relationship for post-trial motions of a jury trial versus a bench trial. We have the detail in our billing systems. It takes time to understand the cost components and correlating relationships. Armed with a thorough understanding of the factors driving costs, we can then utilize fee structures to align the interests of the firm and the client.

I participated in a value exercise recently. The facilitator asked participants to identify products or services they perceive as valuable. One example was a gas station on Fresh Pond Parkway in Cambridge, MA. Typically, Boston commuters only stop with a true need – an empty gas tank. This particular station is full-service with higher prices. Frankly, it's a total hassle to get to, across a very busy road. The service people, however, are courteous and friendly. Even though they don't service your car, they watch out for you; letting you know if your tires look low, or your inspection is about to expire, or fluids are leaking from your engine. They are very busy even though they are inconvenient to get to and expensive compared to other gas stations. Clearly, many customers consider the prices and the inconvenient location worth the value they receive, and will continue to return as long as they maintain their high level of service.

Similarly, firms can set themselves apart from the competition and to some extent deter price pressure, if they can clearly and convincingly demonstrate a higher value to the client.

Risk-sharing fee structures – which are prevalent today – are one way to help do that. In "busted deal" discounting, for example, some firms provide huge discounts to long-term clients if a deal goes south. This might be the extreme, but these "extremists" have developed great client loyalty and large books of business. Good client relationships use continuous risk sharing to provide a greater value benefit. These returns assume structured dialogue at the portfolio or service agreement level and require long-term investments by both clients and their firms.

Unlike busted deal discounts, success fee structures used by the legal profession have always confused me. Almost like doctors, the vast majority of lawyers have their client's best interests at heart. The most successful business people understand that doing more for a client than what is expected keeps that client or business coming back to them as a resource.

Typical success fee structures I see in transactional matters look like this: "We will get the transaction closed by January 31 and for that will recover a 20 percent discount. If we are able to close the transaction by December 31, we will recover any discount and receive a 10 percent success fee." In litigation, it is best to detail the success fee trigger(s) – dismissal of injunction, win on summary judgment, removal of 30 percent of the cases, settlement below $X, or other result that is an "out of the park" result. The success fee can be a percentage of the fee, a percentage of the savings, or fixed dollar amount.

Today we have great opportunities to rework and explore value propositions within our organizations, with our customers, and with our suppliers. By remaining open minded, putting in the effort, developing the skills, and creating new tools we can share the rewards of increased perceived value.

Chapter 4:
Utilizing multiple intelligence sources to create an opportunity scoring assessment

By Patrick Fuller, vice president of business development for Neota Logic, Inc.

Now more than ever, law firms are utilizing a variety of intelligence and research sources to inform the attorneys and staff about their clients, competitors, and their addressable market. Unfortunately, much of the intelligence derived from these sources is siloed, or used in a vacuum. While still valuable, this approach often falls short of fully utilizing the breadth of the information set to power the firm's strategic direction.

It should be noted from the beginning that the most important point for all lawyers to understand is this: everything you and your firm are doing to grow your revenue from existing clients through cross-selling or to land new clients, each and every one of your competitors is doing as well, maybe with greater investments. Adding to this complexity is the client, who is facing greater internal scrutiny around reducing external counsel spend, and is utilizing a bevy of their own consultants in an effort to reduce their spend without increasing risk to the business. Focusing the right resources on the right opportunities, and executing the client and business development strategy efficiently and effectively, are critical to the firm's profitability. This chapter will outline, step-by-step, how to create an Opportunity Scoring Assessment (OSA) that will help you ensure internal resources are channeled into the best opportunities, and that you see the greatest return on that investment.

Setting the foundations – Metrics and scope

One of the first questions firms should ask prior to creating an OSA is how they plan to evaluate the success of the project. This can be answered in a variety of ways, but the two sets of metrics recommended should focus on external win rate and internal cost. By prioritizing opportunities, win rates should improve dramatically. The immediate effect of this will be seen in the reduction of wasted internal resources on opportunities that were not viable to begin with. As part of this initiative, firms should establish a fully loaded cost-per-hour figure for internal resources involved in supporting opportunities, tracking the time spent on each opportunity. Each opportunity should be assigned to applicable attorneys, practice and industry groups, and client teams as well as by client name. This will essentially become the Cost of Goods Sold (COGS) figure that all new revenue can be measured against, by the categories mentioned above as well as additional categories such as known competitors, office location, and more. For firms that invest in legal project management and process improvement education, it will also provide efficiency metrics that can be measured year over year.

Once the internal metrics to be measured are determined, it's time to assess the scope of research capabilities that will be used, and the workflow process that will be used. For the purposes of this article, legal specific intelligence platforms (such as Monitor Suite or AdVantage) will be used, along with a CRM/ERM (customer/enterprise relationship management); the firm's experience database; an external matter, rate, and staffing benchmarking platform; and other traditional research services offered through the typical research providers. In some cases, such as litigation or mergers and acquisitions, there are publicly accessible databases where the data is stored; in others, such as general contract or transactional work, there are no such databases and it is important to gather as much intel as possible from trusted sources.

When setting the scoring values and weighting, consider which factors will be most critical to the decision on which to proceed. For some firms, the ability to perform work at a lower total cost is critical. For others, it may be their experience in specific niches, and for others, it may be the key relationships with certain clients. In some situations, weighting specific criteria may not be needed, or it may be more of a phase two approach to OSA. Most scoring should be fairly simple, utilizing either a 1–5 or 1–10 scale.

With the foundation of the OSA set, now it's time to discuss how the various data sources will be used.

Legal intelligence platforms

The most basic question to start with is: "Who is doing what work for the client and from where?" That's a great start with a number of possibilities, each of which needs to be assessed. Typically, these platforms will provide information on litigation (both state and federal courts), securities and M & A transactions, and IP transactions such as patent prosecution and assignments and trademark registrations.

For firms that may not do a lot of work, for example, in intellectual property (IP) or mergers and acquisitions (M&A), it's still critical to understand which firms are handling those transactions, and where the timekeepers handling those matters are geographically based. A litigation boutique in Chicago may not think twice about trademark registrations, but knowing that a larger general practice firm in Dallas that is often a competitor is handling trademark registrations out of its Birmingham office should be immediately noted.

When looking at outside counsel representation, it is always good to go back around 10 years, and look at the year-on-year trends. How often is the client changing primary outside counsel? Are the same firms showing consistently, or is there a variety of firms? What size of firm does the client typically hire for certain types of matters, such as commercial litigation or general liability matters? Does the client hire boutique firms for IP and employment matters? For litigation, are certain firms representing the client in multiple jurisdictions and geographies on a regular basis? It is also important to compare the client's volume and type of work, especially around litigation, with that of their industry or key competitors. Does this client tend to have a higher or lower volume of litigation, for example, than their rivals?

Most of these platforms will also show the individual firm offices that are utilized, based upon the location of the attorneys named in the documents. This is important to note for pricing purposes. For example, if Firm A is based in Chicago, but typically handles an average of 15 of Client X's 20 wage and hour disputes per year out of their Los Angeles office, primarily in California but also in neighboring states, it needs to be noted. It's also important, for experience purposes, to note the opposing counsel for the client, especially if a pattern emerges, as well any judges that are often assigned to cases involving the client.

This is all made easier, with practice areas such as litigation, where there are numerous databases from which to extract information. For general transactional or legal areas where database searching is not available, it is important to gather as much of this information as possible.

The primary questions that need to be addressed in this section relate to the likelihood of the client changing outside counsel, as well as assessing any competitive advantage the firm or attorneys may have against the incumbent counsel or probable competitors. This is where assessing the other touch points competing firms have becomes important. Does our competition already have a relationship with this potential client? As a result, here are the three questions to score for this section:

1. What is the likelihood the client will change counsel?
2. Are we positioned well to compete for the business?
3. Is there potential to grow the relationship with this client?

Relationships and connections

There's an old saying that the only two things that a law firm can truly call their own are their relationships and their experience. Both are critical to OSA's, and in similar ways. For relationships, it is critical to understand both the depth and breadth of relationships that the firm has with key decision makers and influencers. Enterprise relationship management (ERM) programs typically catch connections that are not in CRM, as well utilizing various algorithms to assess relationship strength. It is a starting point that is often modified over the course of an OSA, especially as the various stakeholders add context to their relationships in a way that is typically not measured by ERM and CRM systems.

When looking at relationships, the obvious first starting point is to look at who knows whom and how well, for which ERM can provide a baseline. Who has the best relationships with decision-makers, as well as the positive and negative influencers? What can those people in our firm tell us about why each person buys? Ancillary insight into buying motives are typically uncovered here. It is also important to look at the frequency of contact between key stakeholders from both our firm and the client. Has it been a while since the last meaningful contact? Is it consistent? Or have the touch points been inconsistent?

The next area to grade falls under the client's internal political map and relationships. Just like in law firms and virtually every other organization, there are internal politics in corporate legal departments, turf battles with the business, and more. For example, if the goal is to cross-sell employment services to Client A who is mainly a corporate client, it's important to know if the associate general counsel over each section are friendly, competitive, etc. The first rule of strategy when looking to grow revenue is to protect the current base of revenue, so understanding and creating a political map is essential to the relationship scoring section.

Finally, it's helpful to understand competitors' relationships with the key client decision makers and influencers noted previously. Tools like LinkedIn can tell you who is connected to whom (to be clear, that does not always entail a relationship, or even knowing the person), and some of this will come from personal intel gathering, but it's important to understand the relationships that key competitors have as well.

The four questions that are scored here are:

1. The strength of our relationships to the decision makers;
2. The breadth and depth of our relationships with the client;
3. The strength of the internal relationships with the client; and
4. The strength of the relationships competitors have to the decision-makers.

Experience

As noted previously, experience is one of two items unique to all firms. All firms and attorneys have it. The difference is that few do even a good job of collecting and leveraging it for a variety of different uses. Talk to in-house counsel, however, and you'll hear experience as one of the key factors in why firms and attorneys are selected over their competitors. Very few firms utilize their experience for even the most basic client development activities, such as end-of-the-year recaps (and a reminder) on the successes and accomplishments of the previous year, or to help justify rates at a certain level.

In all aspects of business development, whether the focus is on new clients or existing clients, the "3 Es" remain vital: experience, efficiency, and effectiveness.

Experience is a competitive differentiator, plain and simple. Firms that harvest and catalog their experience can more easily teach lawyers how to create demand around this differentiation, utilizing their experience. Earlier in this chapter it was suggested to identify opposing counsel. Having a track record of success and experience against specific counsel can be a very powerful differentiator that separates lawyers and firms from the commodity line of competing or even incumbent firms. While many firms set up alerts with various services on new filings by nature of suit or industry, savvier firms and attorneys also set up alerts on opposing counsel against whom they have a powerful track record.

When scoring experience, the first question is applicability to the client's business and strategy. Is it demonstrable experience, in a narrative or with key facts that the client can assimilate? Can our experience in a certain area lend itself to better budgeting and forecasting for the AGC who is being required to track budgets on a regular basis internally? All of these factors, and more, are critical for scoring this section.

Finally, are the attorneys considered to be subject matter experts in the given area? In addition to the legal work, are there authored articles, books, or key speaking engagements that underscore the "rock star" status the attorney is hoping to project?

The key questions from this section are the following:

1. Can we demonstrate experience, efficiency, and effectiveness in this area?
2. Is our experience a competitive differentiator to the client?
3. Can our experience drive above-average market rates and better margins?

Finance, pricing, and profitability

In any business, focusing on proper margins for every transaction is key to overall profitability. The same is true for the legal profession. Focusing on per-matter profitability, per client profitability, and more is critical to delivering the overall profitability. The first question to be asked is typically: "Is this profitable?" The answer to that question can depend on the staffing mix, discounts, and more.

In an example above, we used Firm A, who as part of their due diligence uncovered that roughly 15 of Company X's wage and hour claims were being handled out of their Los Angeles office. This is important to note, because I can use a variety of rate, matter, and benchmarking sets (all from actual invoices, not surveys) to determine the approximate value of each matter and total average annual value of the opportunity. In this example, Firm A is an Am Law 100 firm, and from the data sets examined, roughly 80 percent of all wage and hour claims analyzed that were billed by Am Law 100 firms out of their Los Angeles office closed with between 700–1,000 billable hours, with a weighted mean of $205,000.[1] So, if Company X is averaging 15 of these matters annually, billed out of the Los Angeles office of their Am Law 100 outside counsel, the market value of this opportunity is roughly $3.075 million annually. Further, the typical billable rate for these matters, by Am Law 100 firms billing out of Los Angeles, is $560 for partners, and $406 for associates, and associates have historically handled roughly 65 percent of the billable time.

By taking this approach, our firm now understands what the total annual value of the opportunity has been, the price the market will bear per hour, and the staffing mix. This will enable our firm to understand if, based on our COGS, this an opportunity where we can compete financially while still performing profitable work. If the firm decides to propose an alternative fee arrangement to the client, such as a fixed fee proposal, there is data to suggest what the typical fees for such matters generate by peer firms, and the staffing mix can be adjusted to ensure optimal margins. The question to ask from this section: Can we perform this work profitably?

Once all the data sections have been scored, simply add up the points. If a firm is weighting any particular criteria, account for that as part of the scoring. This presents a very simple way of prioritizing which opportunities are pursued first. The key to this, as always, is not to let desired outcomes influence the scoring; that is to say, do not let the subjective influence the objective.

Reference

1. Source: ELM Solutions LegalVIEW Database.

Chapter 5:
Developing a CI function in a resource-constrained environment

By Annie Johnson, manager of business intelligence at Pillsbury Winthrop Shaw Pittman

It is no surprise that law firms are operating in an increasingly cost-sensitive environment, where buzz-words such as "value-add" and "alternative fees" have become part of the everyday vernacular. It is a universe of dichotomy; clients want to save money and lawyers want to make money.

In a 2014 report from Altman Weil, a majority of law firms surveyed agreed that factors such as price competition, commoditization of legal work, and the onslaught of non-traditional service providers were permanent fixtures on the new legal landscape. In addition to stagnant demand and pricing pressures, that means the legal industry is watching savvy new providers snap up work.

It is challenging to operate as support staff in such an environment. But winning the hearts (and wallets) of managing partners and chiefs and senior directors is largely about changing the way we think. Competitive intelligence is not a line item. It is not a budget allocation. It is value service that drives revenue and gives you a leg-up on the myriad law firms and attorneys that know very little about what their clients actually do.

It's a mentality that can be applied whether you're looking to add to a growing roster of CI analysts and professionals or simply looking to get your department off the ground.

Gaining buy-in

The first component of supporting that money-making mentality is making the case for demand. This is where preparation and data come into play. Just as an attorneys would prep to pitch major Fortune 500 companies, so it should be on the journey seeking additional resources.

The first – and most difficult step – is using data to establish need. Whether there's already a formal request process for business research and analysis, or the firm is looking to put one in place, be sure to collect as much data as is feasible. Borrowing a page out of journalism's textbooks, gaining buy-in should start with at least three months of data regarding the who, what, when, and how much of information requests. If there is not yet a central repository for such information, consider tapping the firm's information services team, business developers, and even financial analysts to get a sense of which attorneys are requesting what information and from whom.

This is not a statistics or economics equation; the goal is in fact to illustrate need across multiple departments and attorneys. Are there certain practice sections that require information more than others? Are there individual high-billing attorneys looking for support across major pitches? What is total demand? And, if possible, how much staff time (i.e. non-billable) is spent on doing such work?

The advantage of collecting data is twofold; it quantifies need and can help determine attorney and staff champions. Those champions will be helping support the need for additional resources and each of them has different skin in the game. Take the time to understand that bias. In most instances, the prized possession of such individuals is time. Will an additional resource allow a firm librarian to spend more time on billable requests? Will a new CI function allow a business developer to refocus efforts on creating a new focus team? Can a new CI analyst make room for associates to concentrate on client matters as opposed to company research?

Process, process, process

The manufacturing concept of Lean Six Sigma relies on the collaboration of individuals to remove waste from within an organization – literally making it leaner. It is a concept that is now being progressively applied across industries such as healthcare and law and can be applied on a micro level to growing or building a competitive intelligence function.

Process improvement means taking the data dump out of information dissemination. Again, this aligns with the time imperative. Instead of sending 150 pages of SEC filings to an attorney to decipher, pulling out key pieces of information saves time and money and could offer nuggets that might previously have been overlooked.

In other words, take the demand you've spent so long establishing and map out a process for satisfying that need. Here, the CI professional takes data and makes it actionable, providing a centralized resource for information.

"Centralized" is the key word. Law firms, especially larger ones, tend to suffer from major information silos across multiple practices and time zones. In the pitch for additional resources, the process component is the need for structure with an additional benefit. Through centralizing the request process, the CI professional becomes the nerve center of research and analysis – tapping additional resources when necessary and connecting professionals and attorneys when prudent.

Take this made-up but realistic example. Three months ago, a California partner requested monitoring on desalination activities along the coast. Separately, a partner in New York sought information on private equity investors in the water space. If both partners use the same process to request such information, the firm is in position to consider a more holistic, end-to-end offering.

People

There really is no substitute for hard work. Finding, training, and growing CI professionals, particularly at the onset of a new department, can make or break your firm's efforts in this space. All the data and processes in the world won't make up for employees who lack initiative, drive, or creativity. In a resource-constrained environment, this fact becomes amplified.

When hiring external candidates to grow or develop this role, consider those from outside the legal profession with research and analytical skills. An affinity group of CI professionals from a dozen US law firms recently outlined the traits they felt were most important in hiring new CI professionals. Intellectual curiosity, perseverance, resourcefulness, and team spirit were at the top of the list.

There is, however, one way to avoid the pitfalls (personality and money alike) that come with recruiting external candidates: look within. In many law firms, CI responsibilities are already split among a slew of colleagues. By formalizing their involvement and providing training, you've eliminated a potentially detrimental unknown. At one Am Law 100 firm, the CI department is supplemented with staff from the library and client services teams. The "CI focus group" received extensive training on developing insightful company and industry dossiers for dissemination to partners. These colleagues provide support on about half of requests when bandwidth allows. The outcome is win-win: the staff member learns new skills and their departments receive positive firmwide recognition for their role in supporting a new, revenue generating service. By recruiting a handful of these types of personalities (many of whom are seeking professional development opportunities), it is possible to formalize and grow the CI function using existing resources from across the firm.

Take initiative

Your CI department will not create or grow itself. Being unseen and unheard is not uncommon in law firms, particularly in situations where support staff operate from a shared services environment. Building and growing this function requires a bit of pizazz and a willingness to approach various senior leaders with new ideas. We all know law firms aren't exactly hubs of innovation. It's common to hear a lot of "no", "not right now", or the most common "this is how we've always done it". Learning to craft your pitch with data, processes, systems, and people is key, but it's still possible you'll be told "no".

This is where those champions come back into play. Pick your horse. Taking the initiative to build and grow the firm's CI function means approaching certain partners or senior staff and offering a product or service they've not yet seen. In these cases, that product should be polished and refined. Are there target companies on which an attorney or practice group is focused? Is there a particularly adept senior associate that might be interested in formulating plans for the firm to take on legal issues in a bourgeoning area of law? Reading business plans and having conversations with business developers and attorneys can help guide this type of initiative.

Start small. Create a refined newsletter, provide an insightful dossier on a company, ask questions, and solicit feedback. For example, a handful of CI professionals throughout the Am Law 100 provide company briefs as a first step in growing their department. These are one-page documents that provide high-level information on a company (overview, news, outside counsel) prior to a meeting. It is not rocket science. There is no analysis. But lawyers love these documents because they can quickly scan them and gain a better understanding of what is important to a client or prospect. There is no data dump. By knowing what companies or topics are of interest to certain groups of people, the CI professional can offer that "low-hanging" fruit as a helpful introduction to this new service – and it doesn't cost a thing.

Solicit and implement feedback

A little history. Partnerships of more than three lawyers were fairly rare before the Civil War. Commercial pressures forced growth and, by 1898,

25 firms had five lawyers and another 32 had more than five. By 1915, there were 104 firms with five lawyers, and 136 with more than five. "Full service" commercial firms began to appear in centers like New York – firms like the Blatchford (that became Cravath, Swaine & Moore) and Shearman & Sterling. During this time, law firms created a new category of lawyers – associates.

Fast forward to 2016 and things look awfully similar. In fact, the legal industry has continued to grow its business model under the same structure it utilized more than 100 years ago. And so it shouldn't come as a surprise that there will be at least a few colleagues that will work to derail plans or put the kibosh on new ideas.

Make these people part of the process. Solicit their ideas and feedback (which could be negative) and do something with it. Most of the time, these types of colleagues need to feel like they are part of the process, that they came up with a helpful idea – in no uncertain terms, they want to feel useful. That is not to say they will be your greatest cheerleaders. Getting these colleagues to neutral is a more realistic expectation. How would they present information? What publications do they read? What are their thoughts on an emerging industry or legal issue? Once you've collected this feedback, show tangible activity. Implement these ideas to the extent possible. Maybe it's a short newsletter product, or making a minor change to an existing process. You might find that these ideas are among the best and most realistic you'll receive in the course of building the department.

Track outcomes

Show them the money. There is no greater purpose here. And let's be clear about something: competitive intelligence is by no means the sole driver of revenue. There are a million factors that go into winning and expanding work. But consider this: if understanding a client's business makes up a mere five percent of the factors that combine to win new work, one large engagement – or a handful of smaller matters – is likely to pay for your department. This is where that money-making mentality finally shows its colors.

In order for this to become a reality within your CI department, every project, every request, and every small piece of information that goes out the door must be tracked. Say goodbye to the black hole of information. Bid farewell to documents for which you never received feedback. At this stage, your CI department should have a process in place by which data is easily collected. Tracking outcomes is easier if you know the attorneys who are requesting information, the name of the client or target, and whether the data is being used for a pitch or an informal lunch meeting.

There are countless sources of this type of information that your firm might or might not make available. New matter reports, pitch activity reports, and the firm's financial database are just a few options for determining outcomes. The best source of this information, however, always will be people. Relationships with business developers and attorneys can play a key role in tracking outcomes. Consider sending quarterly emails to business developers about the project on which you supported with the goal of reminding them about past and ongoing efforts. Many will likely be thankful for a nudge that they need to check back with an attorney on a focus initiative or target. Ask an attorney how a lunch or pitch meeting went and offer to provide ongoing monitoring on the topic or prospect.

The other benefit to tracking outcomes is measuring time spent and workload. For those departments looking to add staff, this is a key component. How many requests were fielded and by how many people? Law firm CI departments easily field hundreds of these types of requests a year. How is that time spent? On important, analytical revenue-driving efforts? On company briefs for last minute lunch meetings? Which attorneys are requesting information? Often, having high billers as frequent customers can be the only ammunition needed to add staff or purchase new tools.

Ready to launch

Resources will continue to be strained across the legal industry for the foreseeable future. It's a situation that calls for the greatest understanding of a client's needs in many years. Knowing what to offer, when to offer it, and to whom to pitch are an absolute necessity. Just ask Japan's Bridgestone Corp. A lawyer for the company's American unit, speaking at a legal marketing event, told a compelling story about the impact of the Ebola outbreak on the organization. *The Wall Street Journal* – and tons of other media outlets – chronicled how managers huddled around a rubber-tree and googled "Ebola" when the first case arrived at the company's Liberian unit. What followed was a crash course in calming a massive epidemic.

Amid the slew of law firms and attorneys working with Bridgestone, a single attorney from a single law firm reached out to the Bridgestone attorney speaking at this event to commend the company's work in

Africa. Now, that attorney and that law firm are top of mind. It's a simple story about the power of small acts.

Competitive intelligence can unearth and nurture such relationships, whether as a formal function or as a more ad-hoc, though centralized, process. The components to developing such a service are plentiful and varied, though perhaps none is more important than persistence. Developing and growing your firm's CI function might call for a fair bit of trial and error – but as the industry is beginning to understand the importance of change, you just might find a more willing audience than you anticipate.

Chapter 6:
Compiling a useful and user-friendly competitive intelligence report

By Mark A. Gediman, director of information services at Best Best & Krieger LLP

The researched data is now sitting on your computer and you've drawn some interesting conclusions. Now comes the big challenge: communicating this to your audience. Putting together a report is a delicate balancing act between providing enough and too much information, and communicating your conclusions concisely.

Before going through the process step-by-step, I will begin with this caveat: beware the data dump! A data dump consists of bringing together all of the information discovered during the course of your research and just sending it to the requestor. This is done without analysis or thought and usually results in a stack of documents that, when printed, rivals the famed Leaning Tower of Pisa (in this case, a Leaning Tower of Paper). This would require your requestor to spend time they don't have reading this material. It won't happen. Nothing will put off the requestor more than seeing this stack of documents (or multiple email attachments). In fact, you probably won't be asked for another report.

Before you start, it's important to make sure you are tailoring the report to meet a specific purpose. In-depth reports continually struggle between being detailed enough to be useful and becoming a data dump. One of the keys to making it useful lies in the analysis.

So, you've done the research and completed the analysis. Now you have to present this in a format that balances the need to communicate your conclusions while still giving your audience access to the underlying information. There are as many variations to these reports as there are people preparing them. We'll take a look at the process of preparing a report step-by-step, with some discussion as we go along of the important factors that should be considered.

Step 1 – Choice of format

The first choice is the basic report format. Is this an in-depth report or brief thumbnail sketch? Several factors can dictate which way to go. The brief thumbnail is usually a single page long and usually comes with a short turn-around time. This is ironic since the type of information contained in these reports, usually more personal in nature, can be the most difficult to find. This information can include the subject's favorite charities, current business challenges, or shared schooling – the type of information that can be used to connect with a business prospect over lunch, dinner or drinks.

Several years ago, I prepared a brief thumbnail report for an attorney who was meeting with a small business owner over lunch. Among other things, I discovered that the business owner was involved with a local charity. His involvement was very important to him because of an emotional experience he had in his childhood. The attorney's wife was also involved with the same charity, giving the attorney some common ground with the business owner. Think about how powerful it was for the business owner (and prospective client) to discover that the attorney shared his interest. More importantly, he was impressed that the attorney was interested in enough in him and his business to do some research to prepare for the meeting, and said so.

Thumbnail sketches can also be a useful part of the lateral recruiting process. This is an example of how business development tools can have other uses, such as recruiting. These types of reports can help identify the areas where the firm and the prospective attorney have overlapping interests. When you think about it, recruiting an attorney with a book of business is just another type of business development.

Step 2 – The executive summary

Regardless of the type of report, the executive summary is the most important part. Attorneys are the target audience for these documents so it is important to keep in mind how attorneys are used to digesting information when crafting a useful report. Consider that a research memo is organized with the question presented first, the conclusion next and then the discussion. The reader will seldom get to the discussion portion of the memo.

Similarly, make sure the important analytical conclusions are prominently placed and clearly stated. Any important information, such as thumbnail profiles of prospective interviewers, should be included in the executive summary as well. The author of a good report will do well to let this principle guide the preparation of the report.

Remember to keep it as short as possible. For an attorney, time is a precious commodity so the executive summary should be prepared with that in mind. A way of looking at this part of the report is to think of it as a written "elevator speech." A useful guide is to communicate what you would want them to know if you had to explain it to them in elevator as they were heading out to their meeting.

The executive summary portion of the report is not limited to that label. I prefer to call the first page of my report "Things You Should Know" and use colorful graphics to attract the reader's attention. The items that go in this section are the conclusions drawn from the research. It may be a series of bullet points along the lines of:

Opportunity: XYZ Company has been hit with five harassment suits over the past year and half:

- *These harassment suits began soon after a merger was completed.*
- *Areas we can help: Employment advisory services; investigatory services; litigation services.*
- *Useful experience: Partner Smith and Partner Jones helped Client A through a similar situation last year.*

A chart showing the uptick in lawsuits filed against the company over the past five years would be useful in illustrating this event. I love using charts in my reports. Charts are easy to assimilate, they communicate concepts simply, and they keep the look and feel of the report interesting.

The way that your results are communicated is just as important as the research itself. The report should communicate the results in a clear, concise and insightful manner. It should also be interesting enough to grab the reader's attention. Let's face it, an unread report is not only a waste of time and effort; it's also a lost opportunity. A lost opportunity for the firm and for the researcher.

Step 3 – Establish the purpose of the report

The context in which the report is requested is important to consider when putting it together. Keeping this in mind during the preparation of the report ensures that the report is useful and targeted without extraneous clutter. A report looking at a prospective client, for example, is going to look different from one examining an existing client. The factors that should be considered will vary based on the entity that is the subject of the report:

1. Prospective clients

- Response to an RFP:
  - Who are the firm's attorneys in the response team?
  - How does the skill set of the attorneys match with the representation guidelines detailed in the scope of work?
  - What relationships with other firms does this entity currently have?
  - Which of these will likely compete with us for the RFP?
  - What are the typical rates charged by other firms?
  - What makes our firm the best suited for this business?
  - Who will the attorneys be interviewing with?
  - What is the sales history? Trending up or down?
  - Historic litigation analysis (at least five years): types of cases; alignment with firm's strengths.
  - Lunch meeting: philanthropic activities; news items indicating recent challenges (see thumbnail discussion above).

2. Existing clients

- Is the client going to RFP?
  - Why? Possibilities could include dissatisfied with service received from the firm or for financial reasons. For other factors, refer to the RFP factors for prospective clients above.
- Cross-selling opportunities?
  - Identify the services the firm offers that the client is not currently using.
  - Who is providing those services and how do they compare to the firm?
  - Reputation, service, and price are the three basic points of comparison.
  - Remember: this client already is familiar with the firm. Unlike the prospective client, there is no need to introduce the firm. Use the data to show how the client could be taking advantage of the same great service that they have come to depend on to resolve their other issues.

3. Competitors

- Compare their practice with your practice. Consider reputation, rates, and market share.
- Compare their strengths and weaknesses with yours. Consider client training, publications, practice knowledge.
- Volume of lateral moves to and from the competitor firm.
- Are they a possible acquisition target? Do they fill gaps in your practice? (A point to always keep in mind.)

4. Industry sectors

- Industry trends.
- Areas ripe for exploitation (e.g. privacy law).
- What does the future hold? No crystal ball needed. To divine the future, see what the thought leaders are posting on Twitter and in their blogs.[1]

Key points to note

The factors that affect every report are:

- Strategic vision of the firm and practice group: How does this entity fit?
- The practice group making the request: What unique data points will be important to them? For example, the summary for XYZ Company above is clearly written for the labor and employment group.
- The unique interests and personality of the individual requesting the report
- How much time do you have to prepare the report?

Step 4 – Tools

There are also some great tools to use when preparing your report.

SWOT

A popular tool, the classic strengths, weaknesses, opportunities, and threats (SWOT) analysis, is a great way to organize your information and conclusions in a quick, easy-to-read format.[2]

This type of chart can be used to analyze your competitors, the industry, or your firm. A SWOT chart can also be used as a way to compare your firm to a competitor. After you create a SWOT chart for both your firm and the competitor, plot the information using a Venn diagram to visually communicate the areas you differ and the areas that you are similar. This gives an added dimension to the competitor report and visually shows how your firm stacks up to the competition.

Templates

There is some uncertainty concerning the use of templates to prepare competitive intelligence reports. There are a few advantages to using templates. For example, reports produced with them have a uniform look and feel, giving them the appearance of a commodity that can be easily produced on demand. This familiar look and feel aids in promoting the report within the firm.

Templates also have some disadvantages. For example, they lack the flexibility to be adapted when the information doesn't fit nicely into the pre-set structure. They also encourage complacency in the information-gathering process. A tendency may develop to only look for the information contained in the template, causing something interesting to be missed along the way.

Free-form reports

Free form reports also have their good and bad points. First the good. The lack of a format makes it adaptable for any circumstance. The preparer has the freedom to organize the information in whatever manner they feel communicates the information better. There are no restrictions on the thought process of the preparer during the research process since there are well-worn paths to follow. Free form is an extremely flexible method.

Now for the bad. The lack of form and predictability can make these confusing to the requestor. Information is not put in the report in predictable order, which can make it difficult to find. This could create frustration and discourage this individual from requesting another at a later time.

The best report format combines the best of the each option. The predictability of the template combined with the flexibility of the free form report. For example, the executive summary should contain elements that make it engaging to the requestor. These elements should carry from report to report. The report itself should be organized into broad categories (i.e., executive summary, analysis, executives, financials, and news). However, the flexibility to add new information and provide different types of chart is possible within these categories. This gives the requestor the comfort of a familiar product each time with the advantage of unique content.

Tips to make your report stand out

1. Make sure to indicate on the report who prepared it and when. This will reduce the risk that the report will be in use months later. And the attorneys know whom to go to when they need it updated.
2. Save and deliver the report as a read-only pdf. This will protect the information being sent from being inadvertently changed. You can also add bookmarks and links within the documents that will make it easy to navigate.
3. Add a colorful cover page using an image related to the subject of the report.

This will make it easier to identify later on.

Conclusion

A successful report will communicate insightful analysis quickly and intuitively. When producing large in-depth reports, be sure to make your executive summary interesting and brief. The key in any successful report lies in producing a succinct executive summary with a detailed report so it is available should the requestor chose to read it.

References

1. Some excellent blogs can be found at *3Geeks and a Law Blog* (www.geeklawblog.com) and *AuroraWDC* (aurorawdc.com/blog) and by following the twitter feeds of Zena Applebaum (@zappleci), Jan Rivers (@jriversmn), Emily Rushing (@emily_rushing), and Juli Stahl (@jjulistahl), just to name a few.
2. You can find an excellent example of this analysis at: http://isites.harvard.edu/fs/docs/icb.topic1182918.files/MAR %205 %20Slides/SWOT %20Analysis %20Template.pdf.

Chapter 7: Design Thinking and the *why* of BI

By John Alber, futurist at the International Legal Technology Association

Change or die

The decision to implement BI doesn't always get the scrutiny it needs. And the name may have as much to do with it as anything. "Business Intelligence", after all, is such a delectable term, ripe and full, suited to almost any business setting. Take a budget meeting, for example. When asked why you want to spend a half million dollars on a piece of software and still more on implementation and staff, "business intelligence" is an ideal rejoinder. Just serve it up and wait for the cash to follow.

Because who doesn't want to be intelligent about their business? And that desire seems a sufficient end in itself, something that forecloses all further inquiry. So, what better than spending a sizable chunk on BI and throwing up a dashboard – or twenty – as a means of being more… intelligent about your business? Because, obviously, BI means smart.

Beware the obvious. More than most technology investments in business, buying a BI suite needs careful thought at the start, and ongoing attention as it is used. In law, we have only to look around to see why. Many firms have by now invested in CRM and other BI software and staff. But how many can claim to have transformed their relationships with clients or dramatically improved their businesses as a result? Can you name one? Is the delivery of legal services any different as a result?

Truth is, most BI investments are wasted. They produce dashboard eye candy alright. But they don't truly add the kind of intelligence that changes a business's course. And the reason for that is an almost complete lack of attention to the question of why we seek business intelligence in the first place.

We buy BI to *survive*. Today's highly dynamic global marketplace grinds through businesses faster than at any time in the history of business. The average lifespan of a Fortune 500 corporation now may be as little as 15 years. And smaller businesses die sooner. Smaller businesses like law firms?

You would think so. In Big Law, the principle of *stare decisis* applies far beyond legal precedent and well into business practice. Lawyers, we often say, are resistant to change, and perhaps even inimical to it. *Status quo* forever!

So, as Fortune 500 lifespans move from 50 years to as little as 15, why haven't we seen a Big Law extinction event? Perhaps it's because of the insulating effect of the billable hour. That cost-plus business model excuses a lot of obliviousness – and disguises mortality.

But, notwithstanding the billable hour hiatus Big Law has enjoyed, all businesses begin to die the day they are founded, even law firms. And the highest mortality rate arises in those businesses that resolutely stick to their business plans no matter the circumstances. Like Big Law.

Peter Drucker, perhaps the most esteemed management theorist in all of modern business, explains why in his book *Management Challenges for the 21st Century*:

> *"[I]n a period of upheaval, such as the one we are living in, change is the norm. To be sure, it is painful and risky, and above all, it requires a great deal of very hard work. But unless an organization sees that its task is to lead change, that organization – whether a business, a university, or a hospital – will not survive. In a period of rapid structural change the only organizations that survive are the 'change leaders.' It is therefore a central 21st-century challenge for management that its organization become a change leader."*

So, Drucker says, the lesson of businesses in all sectors is *change or die*. Adaptation assures survival.

In the wake of the Great Recession, law *is* in a period of great upheaval. And radical change is rampant, both in the economics of practice and in the how of accomplishing everyday tasks. But that change in the how of practice is not coming from inside the profession; rather almost all significant innovation emanates from outside traditional firms.

Services such as RocketLawyer and LegalZoom are redefining the infrastructure for the delivery of legal services. Virtual entities such as Axiom, Counsel on Call and VLP are reformulating what it means to be a firm. Blockchain-based technologies are restructuring that most basic of legal instrumentalities – the contract – and offering up electronic contracts that are lawyerless, smart and self-enforcing. Alternate dispute resolution services are springing up to remedy the cost, delay and unfairness inherent in an overloaded court system. And all of this is clearly just a beginning. Watson and his yet-to-be-thought-up companions are waiting in the wings.

From all of this, it's clear that law firms of all sizes will have to change too. We've seen that lesson over and over in other industries. Law firms that don't change will get Kodaked, or Blackberried, or Blockbustered. They'll simply fade into irrelevance as the market redefines itself around them. Because *change or die* is the way all business works.

But change how?

Here is where BI pays dividends. Because BI's sweet spot lies precisely in answering questions like "How should we change?" BI is a compass for the business. It helps define the path toward change.

Unfortunately, just buying BI software doesn't automatically create a compass. Someone has to decide what questions to ask, questions that pave the way for change. BI software sometimes comes equipped to ask certain questions. "Are we profitable?" for example. Or even "Where are we profitable?" All it takes is little wiring into existing enterprise systems and those questions can begin to be answered.

And, of course, profitability is one of the core inquiries of any successful business. But just how well does profitability or unprofitability answer the question "Where shall we change?" It may begin an inquiry, but it by no means ends it.

Design thinking discipline

So if BI software can't answer the most important questions right out of the box, how do business leaders in general and BI analysts in particular begin to know what questions to ask to lay in a path for change? How do they even know where to start?

Just as there is a discipline to parsing data, understanding data distributions and undertaking regression analyses, there is also a discipline to designing or redesigning a business. And that is exactly what BI undertakes to do. When we ask what needs to change, we are by definition designing something to take the place of the *status quo*.

And there is a discipline to design that we can make use of in asking these fundamental questions. Over the past several decades, businesses have begun to notice that professionals in design fields – architects, urban planners, industrial designers, and other "creative" types – solve problems in a fundamentally different way than scientists, businesspeople and lawyers. They exert just as much discipline as more conventional analytical thinkers, but often wind up in very different, and much more productive, places. Design Thinking, as it has come to be called, is a translation of the methods used by the most successful designers into language that can be applied in other settings.

Design Thinking is a catchy name, but a little misleading, given our understanding of the term "design." When we speak of design, we often attach an article to it, referring to "a" particular design as being beautiful, or elegant. The smooth metallic surface and radiused edges of the iPhone, for example, fit that understanding of design. In that sense, design refers to a particular physical aesthetic and it seems to fall far outside realms like business and law.

But design is also a process, a methodology used to arrive at a superior end state. And it goes far beyond the physical aesthetics of product creation to encompass the entire user experience associated with a product or service.

As attractive as the iPhone's physical design was, the revolution it spawned had much more to do with how users interacted with a wide range of services, from telephony, to email to music to photography and videography.

And to get to *that* required a most extraordinary kind of inquiry. Because had you asked conventional phone users whether they needed something like the iPhone, they would have said no. They might have quarreled with this or that bit of functionality in their phones, but they were not asking for iPhones.

To get to the iPhone, something else had to happen during the design. This "something else," this way of inquiring that is so different from the way in which businesspeople and lawyers typically approach problems, can prove revolutionary when applied to business problems. And, more particularly, it can serve as an underpinning for the ever-present BI questions: "What shall we measure?" and "What shall we change?"

Empathy?

At the core of Design Thinking is something utterly outside the toolset given lawyers in law school and businesspeople in business school – empathy. Empathy goes beyond simply trying to understand a problem. It asks you to put yourself in the shoes of the person who will use your product or service, and to try to understand that person in ways that transcend logic, that draw upon intuition and emotion as well.

Design Thinking recognizes the first-level importance of the emotional content of a successful design. When we think of traditional value propositions, we often bring to mind some emotionless notion of utility. This product or service will accomplish a certain thing. Lawyers think like that. We will provide you with advice, and it will be correct. BI analysts think like that too. We will tell you your billing speed and collection speed and it will be correct.

But the most successful designs go beyond mere utility. If you buy a Tesla, the automaker promises that you will receive the safest transportation in the world, that you will be transported in a sumptuous surround, that you will feel pampered, affluent, and intelligent. In other words, the design of a Tesla is loaded with emotional content. So too with the iPhone. Its hip exclusivity is as much a part of the design as its elegant user interface. All of the best designs are founded first on human considerations.

Clients have been telling us for years that they want more than utility in their law firms. One of the most common complaints about lawyers is that they take no time to understand their clients' businesses. That complaint certainly relates to the utility of advice – abstract advice is less valuable than that given in a specific business context. But the complaint also has just as much emotional content as a "you don't pay enough attention to me" statement in any other human relationship.

That untapped resource, the as yet unasked questions that open up the workings of our clients' businesses, presents an extraordinary opportunity for BI. Helping lawyers understand their clients' businesses, or even better, helping clients themselves better understand their businesses, represents the foremost opportunity of BI in law.

Bringing empathy to BI

So, what might it look like to begin applying Design Thinking to the question of how to use BI to improve the delivery of legal services?

First, let's get this out of the way. There's some work involved. As you might expect with any discipline, there is a good deal of structure to Design Thinking and a real learning curve. And you'll need to work your way up that curve. A good way to get started is to use the resources compiled by the Stanford Design School, one of the leading proponents of Design Thinking in the technology sector. Stanford's D School is especially influential on designs emerging from Silicon Valley. The D School's *Bootcamp Bootleg* will get you off and running in applying Design Thinking to your work.

But before we do all that work can we test run what empathy-based design feels like? Sure! One of the most approachable answers to that question comes from Warren Berger, who in the Harvard Business Review's *The Four Phases of Design Thinking* describes the sort of mental states that arise during Design Thinking. Berger's observations, arrived at after consulting with and watching closely as over a hundred designers did their work, nicely deconstruct empathy and summarize the ensuing design steps. To quote Berger, when you do Design Thinking successfully, you do four things:

> *"Question. If you spend any time around designers, you quickly discover this about them: They ask, and raise, a lot of questions. Often this is the starting point in the design process, and it can have a profound influence on everything that follows. Many of the designers I studied … talked about the importance of asking 'stupid questions' – the ones that challenge the existing realities and assumptions in a given industry or sector. The persistent tendency of designers to do this is captured in the joke designers tell about themselves. How many designers does it take to change a light bulb? Answer: Does it have to be a light bulb?"*

Berger notes that it can be particularly difficult to ask those "stupid" questions, because they can make the questioner seem naïve. And he wasn't talking about lawyers, who may be more skeptical and cynical than the average business person. Lawyers, he might agree, constitute the Design Thinking acid test. But skeptics and cynics or not, Berger emphasizes that the telling question is the heart of Design Thinking. So summon your courage and get to the soul of the matter. Be willing to ask even the most fundamental questions, ones as fundamental as "What business are we in?"

> *"Care. Focus groups and questionnaires don't cut it; designers know that you must care enough to actually be present in people's lives."*

Berger's second step urges you to care enough about the problems your users face to get out of your cube or office and meet them face-to-face. And this is more than a matter of commitment. Unless you're physically present, you can't pick up the non-verbal clues to meaning that are so essential to Design Thinking. You can't see that people are pretty frustrated with their flip-phones and Blackberrys and that some other kind of interface might help them.

"Connect. Designers know that you must 'think laterally' – searching far and wide for ideas and influences – and must also be willing to try connecting ideas that might not seem to go together. This is a way of thinking that can also be embraced by non-designers."

Berger says that connecting ideas is a shortcut to innovation. You can meet users' needs without inventing a solution from scratch. Here again, the iPhone is a model of connection. The email, telephony and other services it embodied were not new, but they were *connected* in a new way.

"Commit. It's one thing to dream up original ideas. But designers quickly take those ideas beyond the realm of imagination by giving form to them. Whether it's a napkin sketch, a prototype carved from foam rubber, or a digital mock-up, the quick-and-rough models that designers constantly create are a critical component of innovation – because when you give form to an idea, you begin to make it real."

Committing early raises the specter of failure, because early designs have rough edges. They may even head off in the wrong direction. But Berger notes that committed designers cultivate a tolerance for failure, because they know that failure is on the path to success. They're committed to fully meeting the needs that they uncover in the course of their empathetic inquiry.

Lawyers, of course, are trained *never* to fail, which means that you may need a deeper level of commitment to endure the skepticism lawyers bring to napkin sketches and other rough ideas. So commit with a vengeance!

OMG

If you're a normal BI professional, by this point in the chapter, you should be thinking "OMG, what have I gotten myself into? Let's just screw in the damn light bulb, OK?" But stay with Design Thinking a little longer to see where it might lead.

We see from Berger that the fundamental thrust of Design Thinking concerns getting to the smart question, the really telling question. And the most telling question might appear at first to be a dumb question. But you can't get deeply into somebody's life without dropping assumptions and presumptions and just asking about what you don't know. And these most fundamental questions aren't dumb, because at the foundational levels of someone else's work, you *can't* know without abandoning your ego and asking very, very basic things.

Beginning with the prosaic

OK, so we've gotten a rough feel for the "telling question" approach of Design Thinking. How does it work in practice? We could throw you off into the deep end, right at an inquiry that goes to the heart of law practice. But let's start with something simpler first. We'll begin with the truly prosaic – a business measure likely to be found inside many law firms – and work some Design Thinking on it to see what happens. As we do this, we'll be shortcutting a good deal. We can't trace all the question taxonomies that are necessary to elicit these results. Moreover, Design Thinking goes far beyond merely asking questions of interviewees, and includes the close observation of subjects to capture important verbal and nonverbal clues to deeply held beliefs. But these questions will give you the idea how Design Thinking inquiry flows and just how far you can get by starting with "dumb" questions.

Bill speed is as prosaic a measure as we're likely to find. It's the number of days it takes a lawyer, on average, to issue a bill after work is done on accounts he or she bills for. Now, there are probably a dozen different ways to handle the nuances of bill speed. But why don't we skip that? And you can throw up bill speed on your dashboards any number of ways. Should you use a speedometer dial? Because we're measuring bill *speed*! Clever, right? Or not, so maybe a bar graph? Let's skip that too.

Instead, why don't we begin looking for the telling questions about bill speed? Like, *why* do we measure bill speed? Is that a "dumb" enough question to qualify for Design Thinking? It's a starting point, anyway – an entrée into the bill speed question taxonomy.

Note that here we are directing questions towards ourselves. Doing full scale Design Thinking, we would extend the inquiries deeply into the user population and "pay no attention to the man behind the curtain." But to get a feel for the kinds of questions that flow from Design Thinking, these "thought experiments" on ourselves will do for now.

So, again, why do we measure bill speed? Is it because it's important to revenue streams? Indeed, to push the inquiry, might we do a little research or maybe even examine our own data, to find if there is a correlation between the speed with which a bill is issued and the percentage of the bill that gets paid. If you bill sooner do you get paid more? Do we measure bill speed because we want to reduce it and thereby increase revenues?

If you're good at BI, these questions are probably natural and you work through them all the time with different measures. But you can go much further using Design Thinking techniques.

For example, who is the bill speed measure meant for? Upper management, right? They're probably the one who asked for it. But is it really for them? Why, again, are we measuring bill speed?

Aren't we really trying to influence the behavior of those lawyers who prepare the draft bills, to get them to do it faster? So, we care about what's in their head, right? Design Thinking would tell us they're the real customer here, so we should be inquiring about their emotional state, their deepest feelings and beliefs. *They're* the ones we really ought to be interviewing.

We can go a long way plumbing the depths of lawyer experience. And, in the limited space of this chapter, we don't have time to work through all the possible questions we might ask, much less actually chronicle the interviews. So let's cut to the chase. Here's what you'll find if you *do* do those interviews.

After we got deeply enough into lawyer headspace, we'd find that law school was a fiercely competitive grind and that it has left a permanent mark. It both preselected candidates who are sensitive to relative positions in their cohort and it further conditioned graduates to be even more sensitive to relative rank. We would see high levels of sensitivity in connection with LSAT rankings while applying for school, in class rankings during school, and in the most certain ranking method found inside law firms after school is done – compensation. Not all lawyers are driven to maximize compensation. But a close enough study of lawyers would reveal that all are attuned to their relative rank in the firm, just as they were in law school. Once you bang around in lawyer heads long enough, you can see that relative rank evokes powerful emotions and can therefore act as a powerful force for change.

And understanding that about lawyers gives you another question to ask. In influencing lawyers to change habits like bill speed, what if we measured in relative terms, just as was done with the LSAT and in law school? What if we measured bill speed in, say, percentiles, with the fastest lawyers in the highest percentile rankings? Might that make a strong emotional connection with our users, something strong enough to influence behavior?

That's the kind of question that lets you begin an experiment – exactly the kind of experiment contemplated by Design Thinking. What you may find, if your lawyers are like the lawyers at the firm where we tried this experiment, is that relative ranking is a very direct way into the heads and hearts of lawyers. They care about it and will change behavior significantly to alter rankings. In our experiment, while absolute measures of bill speed remained essentially unchanged for years, relative ranking improved firm wide bill speed averages by more than seven days within the span of six months. And that drops money to the bottom line, both as a function of the time value of money and of increased collections percentages. Using empathy to find emotional tipping points pays.

This example is not to tout a particular way to measure bill speed. Rather, it illustrates the process by which that way of measuring was arrived at. And note that empathy doesn't always mean doing something a customer wants. Remember, no one was asking for iPhones and no lawyers were asking for relative rankings. But empathy does entail getting as deeply into the point of view of your subject as possible – *becoming* them in some sense of the word. And that skill has as much a place in BI as it does in any design discipline. Indeed, if it's not present in BI, it may be that you only wind up measuring things you can't change.

Back to the why of BI

We don't think of bill speed as a *change or die* proposition. Well, maybe – if your firm bills so slowly it's in danger of starvation. But remember, we were talking about questions that go to the heart of the delivery of legal services. What might applying Design Thinking to those most fundamental propositions look like?

Let's start with a *really* stupid question, one that's highly likely to provoke acerbic responses from the lawyers themselves, particularly if you're senior enough that they think you should know this.

What does a lawyer do?

I would contend that question is so basic that even most lawyers can't answer it, because they think they already know the answer. If you asked a lawyer "What do you do?" They might say something like "I represent high technology companies in the acquisition and protection of their assets," or "I litigate complex disputes, mainly in the financial sector."

And those answers would be right, but they're incomplete. They certainly don't go far enough to give you any hint as to what you might begin measuring to foster needed change.

So, again, what do lawyers do? If you worked your way through all the firm lawyers and back to a law department, you might get a different answer about what outside lawyers do for the companies they represent. A law department lawyer might say that outside law firms help them avoid problems and manage the problems that do occur. And by problems, mostly law departments mean lawsuits, regulatory hurdles and the like. Those are the day-to-day concerns of in-house lawyers. They might also say that outside lawyers spend their company's money.

Legal spend, you must know, is something everyone measures, inside and outside lawyers alike. But you can go much deeper than that and begin to get to real meaning.

Once you plunge deep inside a corporation, away from lawyers altogether and into the heads of those who create strategies for our corporate clients, you begin to get at what lawyers *really* do. A Peter Drucker-trained manager might say that lawyers help companies manage risk. Every day businesses continually encounter, create, trade and arbitrage risks. In some senses, risks are the real currency of business. As Ducker said:

> *"Strategic planning is the continuous process of making present entrepreneurial (risk-taking) decisions systematically and with the greatest knowledge of their futurity; organizing systematically the efforts needed to carry out these decisions; and measuring the results of these decisions against the expectations through organized, systematic feedback."*

Notice how central information gathering and measurement are to the management of entrepreneurial risks. Those are BI functions and they need not stop at the boundaries of the corporation. Indeed, because lawyers help companies manage risks, it would seem imperative that law firms also measure their impact on pools of risk.

We see some firms beginning to do this when handling large litigation portfolios, mainly in the financial sector. The notion of "risk weighted exposure" is an effort to arrive at a present value risk exposure for a single suit all the way up through an entire portfolio.

That's an important undertaking in that it permits the client corporation to make large-scale decisions in the process of managing risk. Once it is quantified, risk can be leveraged, hedged or mitigated in any number of ways.

And here again, law firms who ask stupid questions can begin to aid the corporation in managing risks. Here's a stupid question you might ask: "As against a multi-billion dollar portfolio of risk weighted exposure, are there any causes of action, defenses or counterclaims that markedly increase exposure out of normal ranges?"

Experience shows that, at least in some portfolios, the answer is yes. Some defenses, for example, have out-of-scale impacts on both cost and schedule. And that bears on the type of legal advice a firm might want to offer. If fraud counterclaims or defenses have an extraordinary impact on cost, might a firm consider *not* raising every colorable fraud claim it encounters?

Apply that kind of filter across an entire portfolio and a firm might begin to reduce overall risk-weighted exposure by significant amounts. Similar approaches might work after running regression analyses against deal terms and litigations, or various regulatory undertakings. And all of this arises from the question of what lawyers do.

The simplest questions, the stupidest, if you will, are the ones that present the most opportunity. And the canvas is still largely blank, waiting for a BI artist to finally do something transformational to the relationship between lawyer and client. All you have to be willing to do is think like a designer, and ask stupid questions.

It may be that you're not in a position now to take questions all the way past the law department and to high officers inside client corporations. But you can begin applying a Design Thinking methodology even on the most prosaic measures and achieve sometimes stunning results. The key is to be willing to venture past yourself and your own cohort and delve deeply into the heads and hearts of the people you most need to understand.

The key is empathy. And it unlocks transformational change.

Chapter 8:
From BI to AI

By Joanna Goodman, freelance journalist and IT columnist for the Law Society Gazette *and the* Guardian; *author of* Robots in Law *(ARK Group, 2016)*

Legal AI is more than applying mathematical forecasting techniques to real-time data. This chapter looks at the journey from business intelligence (BI) to artificial intelligence (AI) and how mainstream technology offerings related to data capture and analysis provide a jumping off point for legal AI.

It is said, "if you can't measure it, you can't manage it," and legal practice management has for some time focused on capturing management information in real time and presenting in a way that provides insights into the business and opportunities to improve productivity and performance. Popular legal practice management systems including LexisNexis, Thomson Reuters Elite, Aderant, and Peppermint feature BI capability. Specialist BI software provided by C24, DW Reporting, and QlikView among others captures financial and performance metrics from across the business and presents them back to management and fee-earners in real time, highlighting progress against key performance indicators and guiding decision making. BI, data analysis, and content management are the foundations of legal AI.

Law firms are for-profit organisations, so leveraging management information is a key driver of BI. Financial data is presented in a way that identifies which matters, clients and sectors are most profitable, and which lawyers are recording the highest number of billable hours and earning the most money for the firm. Client billing and other data can inform business development and client relationship management. Business intelligence supports classic management techniques including business process management, Lean Six Sigma, and agile working, which boost productivity and efficiency by identifying and dealing with bottlenecks as well as highlighting best practices and rolling them out across the business.

An important benefit of BI is that the data can be broken down in a multitude of ways to support different roles – for example, fee-earners can look at their own billing by matter, over time, and against their targets and compare their performance with others, whereas a partner leading a practice area could look at billing or other indicators for their whole department and then break it down by sector, matter, client, team, or fee-earner. Business support departments such as finance, HR, or business development would focus on different metrics according to their strategic priorities.

The BI "dashboard" is tailored to the user's profile and gives them an "at a glance" overview of the firm's key metrics. Lawyers can then drill down into the data to discover, for example, how they or their team or department are doing compared with a previous time period, their peers, or other benchmarks determined by the firm's system. BI applications can be configured to identify common business issues and potential solutions.

BI and big data

More recently law firms have been leveraging external data too. This is less about business efficiency, and more about supporting strategic decision-making in a more outward-facing way than BI. Big data was the legal IT buzzword that preceded innovation and AI – and it is now part of the law firm technology architecture to the extent that some larger law firms employ business analysts and data scientists. Big data analytics apply complex algorithms to large anonymised data sets which are cut and combined in different ways to identify patterns, highlight opportunities and risks and predict trends. In the past few years, firms have been applying big data analytics to legal work, often with the aim of minimising risk and identifying expertise.

Although the obvious differentiator is volume, big data analytics is commonly described as comprising five Vs: volume, variety, velocity, veracity, and visualisation. A sixth feature that is particularly relevant to law firms (in terms of investment decisions and partner involvement as well as market intelligence and business performance) is value. Because big data analysis requires specialist tools and applications that are designed to analyse large volumes of data quickly and effectively and present the outputs in a meaningful way as well as specific skillsets, law firm (and ABS) decision makers need to be able to demonstrate to partners and stakeholders how it will produce a return on investment (ROI) in relation to improving productivity, winning cases, expanding client services, and boosting margins. These value considerations apply equally to legal AI.

Although BI and big data analytics combine data from various sources to support strategic and operational decision making, there are important differences relating to their positioning in the business. Derek Southall, head of innovation and digital at Gowling WLG, extends the dashboard imagery by describing BI as the firm's speedometer – an essential indicator that presents internal structured data back to those who are driving the business in real time. Southall is among those who believe that law firms are only just getting to grips with BI.

Whereas BI applications analyse and present financial and management information from multiple repositories and perspectives within the business, big data analytics relate the firm's strategic direction and planning to external factors – the business environment and customer behaviour. The data, which can include internal management information as well as transactional and customer data and data from external sources, can be cut in different ways – i.e. by geography, market, sector or product or any combination – depending on the purpose of the exercise. Continuing Southall's analogy, where BI is the speedometer, measuring performance in real time, big data analytics is the satnav that shows you where you are in relation to your environment and the weight of traffic around you, keeps a record of recent journeys and helps you decide on the best route to your destination!

Big data analytics have been applied successfully to volume legal services. For example, at DWF a team of analysts use big data software to identify potentially fraudulent insurance claims. BLM applies big data analytics to claims data, and feeds back the findings directly to its insurance clients.

Data visualisation, which is a graphical representation of large volume data patterns, is an important part of big data analytics. Like BI's dashboards, the purpose is to make the results of the analysis easy to access and understand, which it certainly is in comparison with spreadsheets!

In 2014, Wright Hassall IT director Martyn Wells introduced C24's Bi24 business intelligence and analytics platform to support the firm's debt recovery business. A geo-demographic heat map identifies which locations have a higher propensity to pay and the recovery team concentrates its efforts on these areas, significantly improving its success rates. This drives decision making on how to proceed with particular cases – there is not much point in pursuing a case that is unlikely to produce results.

A blend of big data analytics and BI guide Wright Hassall's strategic decision-making around expansion and process improvement, by applying big data techniques to industry areas in which the firm operates – and new ones it is considering moving into. The BI platform handles natural language queries (a key element of AI) to identify data clusters – for example, how many conveyancing instructions the firm is handling. Users can then drill down into the detail, splitting the data by location, property type, price etc. While client dashboards give clients real-time access to the progress of their matters, data analytics are also applied to internal processes to identify bottlenecks, prevent the build-of WIP and lock-in, and support work allocation and team management.

Big data analytics are used to identify patterns and trends in dispute resolution to predict the probability of case outcomes. In the US, LexisNexis Lex Machina applies analytics to IP transactions and litigation bringing together case information, court records and other public data to predict case outcomes. Toby Unwin's Premonition analyses public data in order to identify the best lawyers to instruct for particular cases – i.e. the ones who have the most experience and the highest success rates.

BI and predictive data analysis, together with advanced search technology, which handles natural language (or close to natural language) queries, are the jumping off point for legal AI because they interrogate large data sets quickly and present the results in way that supports decision making. They support AI, but they are not AI.

AI's two-factor authentication

So what is legal AI? It is worth considering what differentiates AI in the law firm context. It is generally agreed that this comes down to two main applications: machine learning (or cognitive computing) and natural language processing (NLP).

As Peter Wallqvist CEO of RAVN Systems explains, the main difference between BI and AI is that BI applies defined rules to structured data, while AI extracts and interprets unstructured data. As you add more data and rules, the BI system improves – and the quality of output is governed by the accuracy and validity of the data and the clarity of the rules.

"While BI derives insights from cluster analysis or regression analysis and can execute decisions against an algorithm, it cannot learn the consequences of those actions and apply that learning to future decisions," adds Wells at Wright Hassall.

AI applies machine learning to (structured or) unstructured data. Natural language processing (NLP) allows systems to respond to natural language (or close to natural language) queries – i.e. users do not have to use particular search terms and meaning is not defined purely by terminology. The system needs to be trained in the first place – in the same way as a person does – and improves its output by learning from experience and feedback.

RAVN chief technology officer Jan Van Hoecke adds that while BI applies across a firm's business metrics, RAVN's AI-powered Applied Cognitive Engine (ACE) is applied to narrow domains, including AI-powered search, transactional due diligence, commercial contracts, structured finance and banking agreements, and handles discrete contextual tasks which may require recognising a variety of terminology, such as reading through contracts to discover whether they are affected by specific legislative changes. RAVN uses its own technology to identify new domains to extend its patchwork of coverage.

"BI requires data points – to identify which department has the highest billing, or how many hours particular departments or fee-earners put in to achieve a particular outcome or margin," says Van Hoecke. "This means someone has had to identify specific data points such as the number of hours worked and the charge-out rate. BI and big data analysis break down massive data sets to identify patterns and correlations and use visualisation to make them comprehensible. But you still have to interpret the results. AI reads the data and interprets it." He adds that NLP means that data does not have to be classified and machine learning allows the system to interpret the data by applying its training and previous interactions, and then to define a course of action.

BI and big data analytics use data that is structured in terms of meaning, whether or not it is classified – although big data sets are anonymised, some classification is required for big data analytics to produce useful results. For example, medical information will classify patients by gender, age, geography – whichever variables support the purpose of the research. In the commercial world, customer data will be classified by product or service, price and perhaps by payment type or whether something was bought online or in-store.

In the same way, big data applied to legal work is directed at particular practice areas or types of work and the results are interpreted and used to support decision-making. Big data analysis does not interpret the results and define a recommended course of action, although the results may flag up a particular issue or indicate a direction that is likely to achieve the desired outcome. The next step is to add in AI – first to pull together all relevant information to guide decision-making and then to create workflows to apply those decisions.

However, when you introduce AI the algorithm does more than simply apply analytics to data: once the AI engine has been trained to carry out a task, it takes decisions by mimicking what a person would do and applying the appropriate action. Van Hoecke emphasises another important quality – legal AI in particular needs to be good at identifying exceptions, the instances when the AI engine needs to pass on a decision to a lawyer. "It is important that lawyers are confident that the system can provide answers to queries, and take decisions, but that it can also recognise the documents and queries that it cannot handle," he explains. This is another critical difference between BI and AI. RAVN's ACE marks documents that it cannot decide on in a different colour and sends them to a workflow for a lawyer to review. It creates real-time metrics estimating its own accuracy – the percentage of exceptions that it is flagging up. Wallqvist adds that this metric indicates whether it might be worth creating another robot to deal with common exceptions.

At Gowling WLG, Southall agrees that AI is differentiated by the fact that it works with unstructured data. "While BI looks at structured data and gives you the outputs that you require, AI makes sense of random information," he observes. "While there will always be a need for structured data analysis, we're probably going to end up relying less on BI than AI because the amount of unstructured data being produced is phenomenal, exponential and challenging."

The AI of BI – and the BI of AI!

Eric Hunter, director of knowledge, technology and innovation strategies at Bradford & Barthel LLP in San Diego, is blending big data forecasting and predictive analytics with BI to enhance the firm's day-to-day operations. Hunter heads up the firm's spin-off consultancy, Spherical Models, which mines client and case data to predict case outcomes. This facilitates decision-making – for example whether to pursue a case or to settle – and shortens the litigation process allowing the firm to handle more work and price competitively. Visualisation creates a user-friendly interface.

Hunter is working on potentially using AI to add new dimensions to BI, for example by monitoring the tone of communication and recording user preferences in the same way as YouTube does. He explains that adding this new intelligence creates what could be termed "AI-powered BI" "by introducing subtle intelligence that helps ensure the business is going in the right direction – and that is at the heart of BI."

Hunter also underlines the importance of "the BI of AI" – it is critical to monitor the effectiveness of AI applications that incorporate machine learning – in terms of efficiency and their impact on the business. "Machine learning means that we can no longer divorce process from technology," says Hunter. "If we want to achieve something as business leaders, we have to understand precisely how and where new developments impact the business. We need to run BI on AI to make sure it is working towards our strategic and operational objectives."

Get the BI right first

Oz Benamram, chief knowledge officer at White & Case believes that thus far, "robots" in law are a productivity tool – narrow AI that automates routine tasks. "It is still a rules-based engine if it follows a scripted process that involves checking information against particular websites and adding it to a list," he says. "We need to identify the desired outcome beyond automating tasks and work backwards from that. BI will transform into AI when it can connect all the dots in an organisation and help it work towards achieving desirable outcomes beyond automating tasks."

Benamram explains that for a law firm the most significant desired outcome indication is profitability. Like Hunter, he believes that AI could transform BI by focusing on outcomes rather than tasks. "If we can use AI to look at matters collectively and individually and learn commonalities of process and behaviour that increase profitability, we could use this to make high level decisions, like advising a client when to accept negotiation terms. It could also help us with work allocation – for example by indicating that putting a certain associate on a particular case would increase or reduce its chances of success. AI could help us develop true BI related to our overall strategic goal rather than one specific task, by showing us in real time how everything on the way to the desired outcome for each matter will help us or detract us from achieving it. At first we will decide whether or not to act on these indications and forecasts, but as the technology improves, we will use it to manage workflows and write decision trees. As long as people write the rules, it is BI not AI."

At Riverview Law, CEO Karl Chapman's approach reflects this – Riverview's AI-powered virtual assistant KIM works predominantly with structured data, applying knowledge from all parts of the business to different types of legal work. KIM responds to natural language instructions, involves machine learning and can be configured and reconfigured to particular matters. However, KIM also requires a consistent data and context layer. "You have to get the BI right before you can apply AI," says Chapman, explaining that Riverview's system is built up from the data layer. This feels like a further development of legal practice management systems that are based on Microsoft Dynamics – whereby different systems and applications are built on the same underlying database, thereby ensuring data consistency across the business.

This is close to Benamram's vision of AI as a decision making platform predicated on profitability, which would expand BI to all the information related to a matter in order to give it the best possible chance of success. This would change law firm operations by writing the decision tree in real time, while the narrow AI currently in use is changing day-to-day law firm operations and roles through intelligent automation supported by natural language processing and machine learning.

From dashboard to conversation

It has been suggested that narrow AI that incorporates machine learning and natural language processing capability is likely to change the way people interact with BI engines. The rapid results produced by narrow AI systems like RAVN which present their outputs in more direct – and user friendly – ways highlight the option of moving away from the BI dashboard, perhaps to a more conversational user interface. Author and commentator Nir Eyal recently suggested that intelligent software would see the end of the BI dashboard, replacing what he describes as "an intimidating explosion of charts and graphs" with "a conversational interface" that "listens and learns". Although it is unlikely that legal services will abandon the charts and graphs that help them understand the firm's key financial and operational indicators, there is a move towards a conversational interface in the form of the digital virtual assistant.

RAVN's ACE, which undertakes due diligence work, and Riverview's KIM, which is an intelligent knowledge management tool, are among market entrants that apply AI-powered solutions to specific challenges related to managing the volume and content of legal documents. They combine intelligent search with big data analytics, extracting information from the content of large volumes of documents, and there is also an element of BI as context is added to information.

Chapter 9:
URLs or UPL? Using software to close the access to justice gap

By Ed Walters, CEO of Fastcase, and Jeffrey Asjes, research and reference attorney at Fastcase

The United States has a serious and growing problem with access to justice. According to the World Justice Report, the US rates about 47th out of 100 on access to civil justice, one of the lowest scores among high income countries. Prosecuting or defending a civil claim is a dauntingly expensive prospect for the average American citizen. Even for proceedings that stop short of a court appearance, the cost of hiring a lawyer is prohibitive for many, in particular our most vulnerable and disadvantaged citizens. This "access to justice gap" disproportionately affects women, minorities, and immigrant communities. People without legal representation have worse outcomes in domestic violence, housing, and immigration cases, and yet millions of people are forced to face such legal challenges alone. It is important to note that while this article focuses on the US legal market, similar problems with access to justice exist in other countries, and many of the points drawn here will apply elsewhere.

The Legal Services Corporation and legal aid organizations throughout the states struggle to provide low cost representation to lower income clients, but they are collapsing under the burden. Some states have fewer than a single legal aid lawyer for every 10,000 low income residents, and in many states that ratio is getting worse over time. Legal aid is an extremely important safeguard and more effort should undoubtedly be put in to help provide affordable representation to disadvantaged families; however, more than 60 million people are eligible to receive legal aid in the United States. While legal aid is effective on an individual level, it is not a solution that scales well to meet the needs of millions. In addition, hundreds of millions of low- and middle-income families don't qualify for legal aid, but nevertheless can't afford traditional legal services.

Paradoxically, the person-to-person legal services model has created a gaping, unmet demand for legal services.

Mind the gap

The most straightforward way to begin addressing the access to justice gap is to make it easier for people to navigate the legal system without representation. Already this is the approach favored by consumers; according to the American Bar Foundation's Community Needs and Services Study, more than 80 percent of people with legal issues will attempt to resolve their problems by going outside of the formal legal system and will avoid securing representation (many because they don't know that their problem is a legal problem). This kind of self-help is risky; consumers are not legal experts and can easily expose themselves to liability when trying to go it alone.

This is where software comes in. Unlike the traditional approach of attempting to provide more legal aid lawyers, software is scalable. Software can put legal knowledge and expertise directly into the hands of consumers, so that they can help themselves without becoming exposed to further risk, or running afoul of the legal system they are attempting to navigate.

A history of software turbulence

This is not a new concept; other industries with severe scaling problems have already experienced radical shifts as a result of software empowering consumers. In the air travel industry, software revolutionized the relationship between consumers and airlines. In the early days of commercial flight, customers were forced to book via travel agents that specialized in finding (manually, through trial and error) good travel prices and schedules. The ability of an average person to compare prices between different flights and airlines was sharply limited. In the late 1950s, however, software began a revolution in the airline ticketing industry through the introduction of computer reservation systems (CRS). When travel agencies were given access to CRSs, they allowed agents to keep track of all the different flights and prices available at all times, which greatly enhanced the ability of some consumers to make informed decisions – at least the ones who could afford to use travel agents. Then, in the late 1980s, the introduction of travel websites made airline scheduling and pricing information directly accessible to the average consumer. Now, an average person can log on to a website and immediately see the lowest price or fastest flight. Travel agencies have not gone away; they still play an important role in organizing complex travel plans. However, the "simple" cases can now be handled directly by the consumer, more efficiently, faster, and less expensively, without having to go through one of a limited number of experts.

A similar software revolution enabled easier access to stock pricing and trading; allowing consumers to view and understand complex financial information without having to go through a broker. More recently, software has begun to revolutionize the industries as varied as taxis, hospitality, and professional sports. The trend is clear – when an industry has a problem with scalability and access, software can have an enormous impact. The legal industry, with its millions of underserved consumers, is ripe for such a revolution.

Legal software is already here

The legal software revolution is not a distant future concept; it is happening right now. Software is already having an enormous impact on legal practice, and new legal software is being developed all the time. From bankruptcy law, to disputing parking tickets, to advice on interactions with police, software is already being used to make the law more accessible.

One way in which software is enabling greater access to justice is through software products and services that help lawyers represent their clients better, and at a lower cost. Online legal research tools like Fastcase and Google Scholar are allowing small local attorneys instant access to relevant statutes and case law without the time and expense of researching at a physical library. Expert systems such as TopForm and INSZoom help lawyers save time and money when assisting clients with bankruptcy filings and immigration applications, by helping to gather and sort the large amounts of information provided by clients, doing computations behind the scenes with updated laws and regulations, and ensuring that forms are filled out correctly. Meanwhile e-discovery software has vastly decreased the time and expense of a process that once required hundreds, sometimes thousands, of person-hours to complete.

Like the CRS systems from the airline industry, these software systems for lawyers help reduce costs for consumers and increase consumer access to legal information by helping lawyers to do their jobs more easily and efficiently. Just as in the airline industry, however, the next step is to make the legal system directly accessible to consumers. Here, too, software is already having an enormous impact. Companies like TurboTax and LegalZoom allow consumers to fill out complex federal forms and craft their own legal documents for standard applications like lease agreements, wills, trademarks, incorporation documents, and of course, taxes.

Without a lawyer, most people cannot easily craft a lease agreement that will properly protect their interests, or complete a complex local and federal tax filing without making mistakes. Now, through the use of guided software (often called "expert systems", built by software developers with the guidance of lawyers), consumers can craft documents or complete forms in a way that properly protects their interests without requiring the direct assistance of an attorney.

The Georgetown University Law Center now hosts the annual Iron Tech Lawyer Competition, which challenges law students to design and build expert systems to address access to justice problems, often using Neota Logic. Neota Logic empowers legal aid organizations, law firms, and bar associations around the world to create guided knowledge maps and expert systems for law. Neota Logic also has plans to take software-assisted legal aid to the next level through the use of Smart Advisors; artificial intelligence programs designed to intelligently guide users in solving legal problems.

In other countries the trend has taken off as well. In Canada, a new app called Legalswipe provides users with real-time guidance on their legal rights during interactions with police. In the UK, a legal expert system called DoNotPay has helped people access common defenses to beat more than 160,000 traffic tickets at time of writing.

Industry concerns

As software continues to make inroads into the legal services industry, it's not yet clear what the impact will be on legal practitioners. Apps that provide consumers with direct access to the law are excellent for reducing costs and promoting efficiency by allowing consumers to avoid the expense of representation, but lawyers are understandably concerned about the potential for software to render their jobs obsolete. The effects of a revolution like this one are difficult to predict. Like the industrial revolution before it, the software revolution may eliminate some jobs and create entirely new ones. Of course, it's entirely possible that there will be vastly more, or fewer, of the new legal jobs – labor economists completely disagree on this point.

As the legal industry undergoes this revolution, however, it's important to bear in mind that the very existence of the access to justice gap means there is an enormous latent and underserved market for legal services in the United States. By enabling lawyers to begin serving the latent market for legal services in a cost-effective way, the software revolution may end up significantly increasing the number of legal jobs. Regardless of its effect on the legal industry itself, however, the benefits of legal software for consumers is clear – software presents a scalable way to provide low cost legal services to millions of people who could not otherwise afford it.

What's next

Software isn't the future of legal services. Expert systems already assist lawyers, and increasingly their clients directly, in navigating complex areas of law. Software-enhanced legal services are our present.

In many other disciplines, expert systems were just the beginning. Machine learning and artificial intelligence soon followed in disciplines such as logic, finance, and more visibly in complex games such as chess, poker, or Go. Although true machine learning has not yet been applied to law, it is not farfetched to imagine learning classifiers such as logic regression models, native Bayesian learning methods, or genetic algorithms being used to understand large legal collections without the guidance of lawyer editors. Indeed, like Google's Alpha Go software, these legal intelligence engines may not even be able to explain their complex (and ultimately correct) reasoning to lawyers. This raises a serious concern that, as it becomes more advanced, legal software crosses a line from consumer self-help into the unauthorized practice of law (UPL).

Unauthorized practice of law

Statutes in all 50 states protect consumers by requiring that legal services are only delivered by lawyers who have attended an accredited law school, passed the bar exam, and passed a character and fitness review. Similar basic requirements for practicing exist in other countries too. By providing legal information and advice directly to consumers without going through an attorney, it is possible that software services like DoNotPay are "practicing law" without meeting the requirements for doing so. Moreover, as computers get smarter and software becomes more and more capable, machines are likely to encroach further and further into what would traditionally be considered legal practice.

Unclear boundaries

While software *might* violate unauthorized practice rules, however, it is not at all clear which software and which services would do so, and in which jurisdiction. In the United States there is no universal standard for what constitutes "the practice of law". Instead, unauthorized practice rules are set by a patchwork quilt of regulations, state statutes, case law, bar ethics committee opinions, and attorney general opinions. Each state has its own standards and its own understanding of what constitutes unauthorized practice, and those standards are rarely well defined. States generally restrict activities such as representing clients in court, drafting paid legal documents, or signing opinion letters, as the "practice of law", but the rules in each state vary greatly.

The Model Rules of Professional Responsibility Rule 5.5, Comment 2, states the conundrum succinctly: "The definition of the practice of law is established by law and varies from one jurisdiction to another." The Restatement (Third) of the Law Governing Lawyers goes further to say that "the definitions and tests employed by courts to delineate unauthorized practice by nonlawyers have been vague or conclusory, while jurisdictions have differed significantly in describing what constitutes unauthorized practice in particular areas".

For example, in 1997, the Unauthorized Practice of Law Committee of the State Bar of Texas brought suit against Parsons Technology, maker of the CD-ROM Quicken Family Lawyer, claiming that the company's library of computerized, fillable legal forms constituted the practice of law. The court in that case found that the Quicken Family Lawyer program did constitute the unauthorized practice of law, holding that the software purports to select the correct legal form, customizes the document, and "creates an air of reliability about the documents, which increases the likelihood that an individual user will be misled into relying on them".[1] It was only after a lobbying campaign by Parsons Technology that the Texas Legislature amended its UPL statute to make clear that software such as Quicken Family Lawyer did not constitute the practice of law.

Many states, such as New York and Massachusetts, do not consider basic form-filling to be law practice at all, and allow non-lawyers to assist consumers with many forms directly. Others leave ambiguous the determination of when software constitutes UPL.

The lack of clear guidelines and uniformity create a chilling effect on innovation. Software developers can never really know whether they are violating UPL statues in their state. And if they are deemed not to violate the UPL laws of one state, they would still be subject to ambiguous and different UPL statues of the other 49 states, plus the District of Columbia. And this is not an academic concern: the penalties for violating unauthorized practice rules can be severe, ranging from fines to criminal charges. Two-thirds of states have made the unauthorized practice of law a criminal misdemeanor.

So although software has great potential to help close the access to justice gap, the risk of criminal penalties, combined with uncertainty about what is permitted, may well deter many otherwise enthusiastic developers from even trying to enter the market. Thus, in their current (non-standard and ambiguous) form, UPL statutes represent a daunting obstacle to those who would address the access to justice gap with software.

In the face of such a challenge, it is worth reminding ourselves why unauthorized practice rules exist in the first place. UPL rules serve an important purpose of protecting clients from receiving ill-informed or incompetent legal representation. The interest they are designed to protect is that of the consumer in need of sound legal advice, not that of lawyers concerned about disruption in the industry. Of course there is room for legitimate concern that some software companies may have low standards and will provide bad legal advice. Consumers need to be protected against potentially faulty software every bit as much as they need to be protected against unqualified human advisers. Unfortunately, the current system disincentivizes all legal software development, both the good and the bad, because it focuses on who can practice, rather than how they practice.

Inputs vs outputs

It is difficult to directly prevent lawyers from giving incompetent legal advice. State regulators can't be in every courtroom, in every negotiation, or in every late-night legal research session, as lawyers engage in the practice of law. Instead, UPL statutes focus on qualifications; before we allow someone to represent a client's interests in the legal system, we try to ensure that they will navigate that system competently and morally. Lawyers (in most states) must graduate from an accredited law school, must pass a bar exam to prove they have a basic understanding of the law, and must pass a character and fitness exam to prove they have the moral underpinnings to uphold the high standards of the profession for the benefit of clients. In many states, lawyers also are required to keep abreast of changes in the law by attending mandatory continuing legal education.

These requirements do not guarantee that clients receive competent or high quality legal services. But in the absence of regulators at each point of legal service delivery, they set an *ex ante* floor, requiring that anyone licensed to deliver legal services has certain qualifications to do so.

So long as they meet the minimum requirements of licensure, the quality of lawyers' legal work is seldom questioned. A lawyer's practice generally has to reach an extremely low standard before being subject to any form of regulation. As difficult as it is to measure and regulate legal outcomes, the current approach does little to guarantee the quality of legal services provided to clients. Our UPL system measures only the minimum qualification of lawyers (inputs), and ignores completely the quality of legal services provided to clients (outputs).

For one obvious example of the difference between regulating inputs and outputs, the court in *Parsons Tech.* did not analyze whether the forms in Quicken Family Lawyer provided accurate guidance to clients. Although it mattered a great deal to clients, the quality of legal services in Quicken Family Lawyer was immaterial to the court. Following the former UPL statute in Texas, the court only asked whether the software performed services traditionally considered to be the practice of law in Texas (the court held that it did), and whether the software was licensed to practice law (it was not). The court cared about the quality of the inputs, not the quality of the outputs. Unauthorized practice of law statutes are supposed to protect clients, but input-only regulation instead protects the exclusive franchise of lawyers.

This is not to suggest that we should not regulate the profession, or that anyone should be permitted to write legal software. However, if UPL is to fully protect clients (and not just their lawyers), it should consider whether software provides accurate legal advice for the benefit of clients. If software is shown to provide the same or better legal advice than a licensed human attorney, restricting its use will enforce the access to justice gap without a benefit to clients. If our goal is to protect consumers, then we must shift the paradigm from an inputs-focused qualification system to an outputs-focused quality-control system. If a computer can offer sound legal advice, then software companies should be allowed to assist consumers without making their software attend law school and take the bar exam.

A future of robots in the law

The prospect of a computer able to offer competent legal advice does not belong in science fiction. Rather, given the current progress of technology, it is virtually certain that software will be able to deliver some quality legal advice within the next five-to-ten years. Already, computers are driving autonomous cars, performing complex surgeries, and winning at Jeopardy and Go. It is not so far-fetched to picture a computer that can competently draft a boilerplate website privacy policy. As a closed system of information, the law is a field that lends itself to machine learning; a process through which computers recognize patterns in data and apply those patterns to new circumstances. With each passing year, machine learning algorithms get better at a faster rate, and following Moore's Law, the rate of change can be expected to double every two years. It will not be very long before machines are capable of matching or exceeding the performance of human lawyers for some tasks.

Lawyers in the loop

Given the current trajectory of technology in this area, and the enormous unmet need for less expensive legal services, a future without software providing legal advice is becoming increasingly difficult to see. Silicon Valley disruptors would describe legal services as a classic "latent market", characterized by a small clientele served well by legal services, and a yawning, unserved market of people who need professional services, but who are not well served by the incumbent system. If we accept the American Bar Foundation estimate, 80 percent of the market for legal services is unmet, a lucrative hotbed for disruptive innovation.

With such progress on the horizon, there is a danger that if we over-regulate lawyers attempting to work on legal software, or subject lawyers to vague and inconsistent standards for UPL, then non-lawyers will step in to disrupt the market instead. The regulatory framework needs to shift to allow a balance between innovation and client protection – regulating outputs in a way that allows the most clients to gain access to good legal advice. Keep in mind that our objective is to find a regulatory solution that promotes greatest access to quality justice. We currently have (for the most part) quality but not enough access. We can't allow the scale to tip too far in the other direction and promote broad access to middling or low quality legal services. Instead, the goal must be to provide better quality at scale. Legal software will be needed to bridge the access to justice gap, but will require minimum guarantees of quality. Streamlined, harmonized, and clear UPL regulations will create a safe harbor for lawyers to innovate in this area.

We are living in a moment in which lawyers and law firms can direct the future of legal software for the benefit of clients. But if lawyers and law firms do not seize this moment, we can be assured that venture funds and well-funded, for-profit companies certainly will.

Quality service at scale

UPL is not the only mechanism that states can use to protect consumers of legal services. Problems with lawyer-assistance software can be handled through traditional products liability and tort principles, and malpractice insurance can protect lawyers and clients from irreparable harm. We may want to hold software sold directly to consumers to a higher standard than software that is used by lawyers to help their clients. But in both cases, the software company would traditionally be covered by errors and omissions liability insurance (and lawyers, in the latter case, would be covered by malpractice insurance).

Insurance underwriters maintain separate guarantees of quality for information products, and we should expect that, as a matter of loss prevention, they would also wish to certify the accuracy of legal software. Insurers of the future may wish to create a legal software version of Underwriters Laboratories – an organization to set industry standards and test and certify consumer electronics. Regardless of what organization we use to set these standards, the goal is to ensure quality by regulating outputs, rather than qualifications, and 51 disparate UPL regimes are certainly not the only tools we have to protect clients.

Colophon

For a wealthy nation, America has a daunting access to justice problem, and software is one of the only potentially scalable solutions that we can deploy to address it. However, existing UPL regulations may keep lawyers from developing such software. Vague, inconsistent standards in each state make it difficult to know that software hasn't crossed the line to unauthorized practice. UPL has a chilling effect on innovators, and as currently constituted, may hurt the interests of the consumers they are designed to help.

At the same time, software designed to deliver legal services to consumers, or designed to assist lawyers, must meet certain quality standards. Tort or products liability actions may protect clients to some extent, and errors and omissions liability insurance may protect clients, lawyers, and software developers. But to be a truly safe delivery vehicle for legal services, legal software should have to meet quality standards, which will be difficult to enforce with or without consistent UPL guidelines.

Alan Kay, the chief scientist at Atari and a member of the fabled team at Xerox PARC said: "the best way to predict the future is to invent it." Whether lawyers are involved or not, it is hard to imagine that software will not be part of addressing the access to justice gap. Software is eating the world – and law is no different. If we can capture law and expertise in software to solve recurring problems, software can be a major force multiplier for justice. Lawyers should be an important part of this revolution, and standardized, streamlined UPL regulations will help close the access to justice gap, while protecting the integrity of legal services.

The best way to predict the future of legal services is to invent it.

Reference

1. Unauthorized Practice of Law Committee v. Parsons Tech., No. Civ.A.3:97CV-2859H (N.D. Tex., Jan. 22, 1999).

www.ingramcontent.com/pod-product-compliance
Ingram Content Group UK Ltd.
Pitfield, Milton Keynes, MK11 3LW, UK
UKHW021848150926
8657IPUK00005B/143

9 781783 582402